DOWN THE HOLE

A STORY ABOUT DETERMINATION AND COURAGE

BY RICHARD STEWART

Copyright 2021 Richard Stewart

Published by Flyover Books

All rights reserved.
No part of this book may be used or reproduced
in any manner whatsoever without written consent
from the publisher, except for brief quotations for reviews.

If you have questions about this book, you can reach the author at
richardstewartenterprises@outlook.com

FIRST EDITION
10 9 8 7 6 5 4 3 2 1
ISBN: 978-0-6451989-0-4

*To all my friends and family
who have had an impact on my life.*

Introduction

This a story about an Australian miner who, over the last fifteen years, has experienced some extraordinary events in the mining industry in Queensland, Western Australia and parts of the Northern Territory.

My name is Richard J Stewart. I'm known to a lot of my mining colleagues as *Richie Rich* or *The Aceman*. This story involves several of my friends who, with me, have witnessed some extraordinary events from working hard rock underground, gold mining, surface coal, working on the methane gas plants, iron ore fixed plant and iron ore shipping. I will briefly touch on building power stations and maintaining power stations working in the vicinity of 33,000 to 66,000 high voltage switchyards, as well as the dangerous situations we have been close to, minimising the risks and hazards as required by legislation and the Mining and Quarry Acts of all states and territories.

This is a story about determination and courage, having to spend time away from home and flying in and flying out from different mine sites all around the country as a contractor, eventually setting up a business with my young friend. The business is called The Flying Tradesmen and we use an aircraft stationed in the outback mining city Mount Isa in Northwest Queensland Australia, servicing cattle stations and mines both in outback Queensland and Northern Territory.

Again, I want to acknowledge my wife Vijaya, my two daughters Rachel and Cilla, my mining colleagues on all mine sites, and my friends in these townships who at times accommodated me. I am very blessed to have them as friends. I acknowledge my young friend Roy Randal and his family who had a big input into this business.

The resources of Australia are in abundance and have been barely touched. It is a country that is blessed in many ways with golden soil and wealth for toil, as the words of the national anthem say.

Let's not forget the song Australia is well known for:
Once a jolly swagman camped by a billabong
Under the shade of a Coolibah tree
He sang as he watched and waited 'till his Billy boiled
You'll come a waltzing Matilda with me

Waltzing Matilda, waltzing Matilda
You'll come a waltzing Matilda with me
He sang as he watched and waited 'till his Billy boiled
You'll come a waltzing Matilda with me.

There is a great bond between Australia and New Zealand.

Finally, I acknowledge the protection and safety I have through God's grace.

I hope this story will inspire you to never give up on life even when things don't always go right.

The mining industry can be a lonely place, especially when you are away from family and friends for days at a time in remote areas.

This is my story.

The Mount Isa Connection

*I was born to make mistakes
not to fake perfection.*
— DRAKE —

Mount Isa Mines covers an area 62.8 square km (24.2 square miles) and is 1830 km northwest of Brisbane. I had been working at this mine site surface and underground for the last two-and-a-half years for a company contracted to Mount Isa Mines.

My home was the Irish Club Accommodation for that period in Mount Isa, flying back to New Zealand every four weeks with a week off in between. It was the years my daughters were in high school; it was also a time teenage girls needed their father around. At the same time, I was wanting to build a new house for them as we had rented for the previous four years, having left Gisborne on the far east coast of New Zealand. The earnings were greater at the time working remote in outback Northwest Queensland, Australia.

I had to weigh these decisions up with my wife Vijaya and speak to my daughters Rachel and Cilla, as my wife would be a single parent for the four weeks I was away.

Why was the electrical company I had worked and contracted to laying off staff in New Zealand? The government at the time was making decisions to increase company taxes. Companies had threatened to go offshore or threatened to take their products offshore. Eventually they did. Our services were no longer required as these same companies were now having to reduce their costs and downsize all work fronts. I'll leave you to ponder what government we had in at the time. They were not business-friendly.

A New Zealand company was looking for trades people as in electrical instrument fitters, boiler makers and mechanical fitters. We would be increasing the numbers in the Australian work front to help them increase production in the mining industry as Australia was in a mining boom. This would be in copper, lead, zinc, silver, gold, coking coal for making steel, iron ore, nickel etc.

Operations would be surface and underground.

Having been on Mount Isa Mine site now for some time and working near the number two lead concentrator, I would get to see firsthand work fronts that can go wrong. Safety is taken very seriously on all sites and as mentioned mine sites come under the Mining and Quarry Acts, Mining Safety Regulations, and Government Legislation. So, if anything seriously goes wrong, everything is stopped, barricaded off, all tools are left where they are, everyone is removed off site and taken to the nearest crib rooms and briefed. A safety investigation is made, usually involving Occupational Health and Safety personnel as well as the Department of Mines. The Department has electrical, mechanical, chemical, and environmental inspectors and if they find that safety has been seriously breached or if the environment has been seriously damaged, they themselves have the power to close a mine down or suspend operations until adequate measures are taken to improve what has caused the breach.

I will tell you later about a two-hour recorded interview with the mines department on a breach in a high voltage switchyard I was witness to.

A few of the safety management procedures include safety meetings, written job safety analysis on work fronts with input of all persons on that work front, personnel take 5s (which gives you the ability to assess any other hazards that could occur and how you would manage them), and permits to work signed by authorised personnel from the mining company. If you breach them, you can lose your job and be banned from all mining sites for a period of up to five years, depending how serious the breach was. You can also be fined if damage to equipment or injury has occurred due to negligence by you or others working around you.

Safety is taken very seriously as safety officers onsite can pull you up at any time and ask you what safety provisions you have made considering others as well as yourself for the work scope.

Also, drug and alcohol tests are mandatory before going onsite or even randomly done onsite. If onsite you refuse to take a test, this is classed as a failure, and you are automatically removed.

This has happened on several occasions as these persons obviously don't take their work seriously.

In 2006, when I first was onsite at Mount Isa Mines, the mining company was a Swiss company. In 2012, a company called Glencore, a multinational British company with headquarters in Switzerland, bought out Xstrata and mining operations, not only in hard rock but coal mining operations in central Queensland. I will refer to some of these other mines later.

As an electrician I had been working up on the flotation cells when the acid tank exploded. A boiler maker had been welding too close to an acid tank and one spark was enough to cause an explosion. Everyone dropped tools and went running. We all assembled at the emergency assembly point with the emergency siren screaming. No one was hurt fortunately. Immediately, the health and safety team were called in to assess the cause and any implications.

Within two hours, the area where the acid tank was situated was cordoned off and we were back onsite. All the fumes had dissipated, and the area was cleared to work on the expansion.

I had been around when the fitter opened a flange on a cyclone tank as the ore body had clogged the pipe. Trying to release the ore with a steel rod, the ore body suddenly flowed fast, and the rocks came flying out and sliced his face open. He was flown out on an ambulance flight to a major hospital.

Within a two-year period, things were going reasonably smoothly for the production of copper tablets in the copper smelter (which are then trained to the Townsville copper refinery) and lead 8-tonne ingots from the lead smelter (which includes silver). These are also shipped to Townsville by road and rail, then to Europe.

Zinc is also produced from this mine as well as surrounding Glencore mines. All the processed concentrate is sent through to Mount Isa Mines and transported from there.

It was during this two-year period that the number two concentrator was having some major upgrades in the processing plant and any redundant structure or piping was being removed.

A boiler maker with his safety spotter was cutting out some redundant piping. With inadequate fire protection, he proceeded to gas axe cut the piping but didn't allow for the old lagging going up the rise. The safety spotter did not respond quick enough and there was inadequate water prevention to prevent a fire; the lagging went up in flames and caused the main ore belt in the concentrator to catch fire.

The operators in the concentrator were unaware initially what had happened but within minutes, the whole area was engulfed in flames. The emergency sirens went off and everyone in the area was evacuated to the emergency response areas while emergency services and Queensland fire were fighting initially an out-of-control fire.

We were all asked by management if we had anything to do with the cause of the fire as millions of dollars of production and infrastructure had been destroyed.

The fire itself was only controlled after two hours of firefighting.

There would be a big investigation, not only on the health and safety but also Xstrata mining how and why this occurred.

The contracting company with boiler makers was flown off site, never to be heard of again.

As for the number two concentrator, it would take a three-month period to rebuild the damaged infrastructure companies working 24/7 and of course rebuild the international production of processed ore for the international markets.

Things were not all bad on the mine site. I pretty much have worked in most areas on Mount Isa Mines, from the power stations to maintaining and building infrastructure in the high voltage switchyards; replacing and upgrading electrical switch gear in the copper concentrator substations; working in the hazardous areas

replacing specifically designed hazardous rated equipment, all the concentrator and enjoying the Mount Isa scenery in between times which you had to like or hate and want to get out of the area fast as you can. Another fella and I one day got hold of a company ute and decided to take it across country and bowl over termite mounds. If you have never seen termite mounds, come for a visit to far North Queensland and you will see brown infrastructures poking up everywhere from paddocks to sides of the roads. The problem with termites is when they get inside the linings of a house and decide to feast, they eat from the inside out, causing a structure to collapse and the old termite sprayers are called in preferably before this happens.

Getting back to my story with the ute, we tried to plow our way across this open area, driving at about 50 km. We hit one these big termite mounds on impact and sent the ute bouncing backwards. That's how strong some of them are, but we didn't give up. We hit another few smaller ones and they continued to crumble. We then decided to put the vehicle into four-wheel drive and take on some close to vertical slopes. This was working well till we got stuck in a hole and had to lever the wheel out with some bigger rocks. This is the Australian outback where anything that will work goes. Eventually got over the steep rise and came down the other side clearing a bit of scrub and a few more termite mounds. We stopped the ute over on the flat and tried another experiment with these termite mounds. I gave one of the smaller termite mounds a kick with my steel cap boots and nearly broke my toe. Never again and that was the end of our termite mound hunting.

The nights spent at the Irish Club accommodation were not all that bad either. The Irish Club itself is a reasonable size bar restaurant which included two restaurants and a buffet, a night club, a gym pokies, which is not in my fun things to do, and a big outside veranda. When the night club and stage were not operating, I would go and play anything and brass band music as well. Sometimes I would have a private audience just come and listen and sometimes people would just ask me to play.

The funniest thing was one of the other fellas I worked with played the bagpipes and he brought them along one night and was walking up and down the outside balcony playing the world's most annoying instrument, whilst everyone was hooting and hollering. He had a great time. Don't think he got any donations though.

THE MOUNT ISA CONNECTION

There was room for anything that works well in the outback of North Queensland.

There were several of my kiwi countrymen in Mount Isa and at times we would get together on weekends or after work. We had Lake Moondarra, which supplies the water to Mount Isa and the mine. A reasonable size lake that has a dam wall to contain water. Yes, funny enough there are lakes in the dry outback of North Queensland. Lake Julius is another dammed lake 70 km from Mount Isa and is a backup water supply for Mount Isa if Lake Moondarra runs low.

We could swim and eat outdoors, kayak, and boat on and around the lake as temperatures in Queensland especially North Queensland remain consistent all year round. Ranging from extremely hot and humid from October till the end of April (usually anywhere between the upper 30 degrees to low 40s) and from April till October (temp usually in the mid-20s) and in the outback of far North Queensland a chilling wind at night in the winter months. If there was a decent movie, we would even go and watch that on the big screen.

Flies are the curse of the outback and even up north in the Pilbaras of Western Australia. When the sun's out, the flies are up.

There are also freshwater crocodiles around the other side of the lake as well. Crocs are everywhere in North Queensland and the Salties (saltwater crocodiles, very big) can make their way to inland rivers and estuaries. So, you have to be careful where you swim. Crocs aren't particular what they eat.

Apart from crocs, snakes, spiders and box jellyfish on the coastal front, life in Queensland is not too bad.

The distances are great between communities. Mount Isa to Townsville is approximately 1000 km by road and just under two hours by plane directly west, passing through Cloncurry, Julia Creek, Richmond, Hughenden, Charters Towers by road. I have done this mainly by plane and eventually our own aircraft, overnight bus and gone straight to work after the bus stopped at Mount Isa and driven the ten-hour drive to Mount Isa myself.

If you go north from Mount Isa to Darwin crossing the Queensland border into Northern Territory, it's another 1600 km. Townsville to Brisbane is 1600 km roughly and then if travel inland to cross the borders, you will find distances just as great. From East Coast to West Coast of Australia is roughly 4030 km. Distance North to South of Australia is roughly 2437 km. So, you can see Australia has a very big land mass and that landmass is rich in minerals as I have mentioned.

So, Mount Isa was the metropolis of the Queensland outback, a city in the desert identified by two big chimney stacks from the mine. There are also cattle stations in and around Mount Isa spanning thousands of kms. Every August there is a very big Rodeo which Mount Isa hosts and several persons and stock from all over Queensland come and camp and ride their stock.

Rodeo fever and the cowboys are in town showing off their skills in the arena. Bucking bulls, bucking horses, wild woman—all are there.

Always wondered how they made the bulls and horses buck so wildly. I suppose you would if you had your balls strung up tightly as well. Never mind it brings some money and some tourism into the city in the middle of nowhere.

So being in the Isa you can make the most of what they have to offer in the community, enjoying the history from the museum to the underground mine experience to visiting the underground hospital that was carved out during the Second World War due to fear the Japanese would invade the area.

The Gregory National Park is not too far away going north towards Lawn Hill (next to Century Mine). Great river up there and camping facilities or you can go south towards Boulia and watch the Camel races in July or if you are very adventurous you can to the Birdsville horse races in September, 685 km from Mount Isa on the South Australian border. Or you can complain you hate the Isa.

**LIFE IS SHORT, SMILE WHILE YOU HAVE TEETH.
NEVER TRUST PEOPLE WHO SMILE CONSTANTLY.
THEY ARE EITHER SELLING SOMETHING
OR NOT VERY BRIGHT.**

This leads me onto the next part of the Isa journey. Have you ever been caught in a situation where the person you are working with has a frozen smile on his face and you want to wipe it off? Try reverse psychology and put a name to that person you have seen. This imaginary name may identify with a person and that can be really funny.

This happened to be the situation in a switchyard I was overseeing. The civil contractors were building the infrastructure for the blast walls which separated the 33000v transformers from each other. The reason being if one exploded it wouldn't take the other on opposite side out. So, there were about six of these blast walls about 10 m long and 15 m high.

Well, this little fella, the civil supervisor of the concrete and brick wall construction, thought he was the man except I had all the paperwork and working within meters of the 33000v lines was a bit out of his league, but he had this frozen smile. Now I have a good sense of humour and had a name suitable for this fella, a Mr Schneebly (remember from the movie *The School of Rock* with Jack Black). This suited him, he really tried to make this switchyard rock and this name summed him up quite nicely. He wouldn't be the only Mr Schneebly I would come across in later years.

I think the fellas working under him had a bit of a laugh although they never let on about.

There was nearly a situation or two that rose in this switchyard, one being where a trade assistant grabbed a hose and without thinking started spraying the water around the concrete pad to hose down the newly erected blast wall, except what he didn't realise he was also about to spray near the 33000v lines. Immediately I grabbed the hose, pointing it down, and in no uncertain terms gave him a dressing down of the implication of killing himself and endangering the lives of others. Water and HV (high voltage lines) don't go down too well and in a switchyard like that you cannot save anyone except yourself and running out of there is your only choice if an explosion occurs.

I am held responsible for anyone killed, would have the finger pointed at me. Even the paperwork being adhered to wouldn't save me. Prosecutions would follow in a court of law as I was the person responsible for every person authorised to work in that live switchyard, even though designated areas had been isolated for work to be carried out.

The worst thing about it I would lose my electrical licence and therefore my livelihood.

Every day I pray for God's grace and his Angels to protect me and the people I am responsible for.

And all these years he has been there for me. I'm not saying things don't happen out of my control, but he has kept me safe and the persons I am responsible for protected.

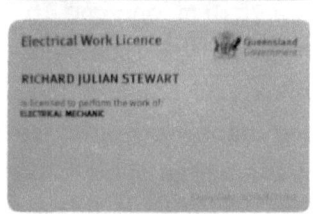

The second incident was when *Mr Scheebly* decided to bring an aluminium extension ladder into the switchyard. Again, power-lines and a metal conductor, not a good combination. This time I had to call the engineer in to control this fella. Big Steve gave him the dressing down and was a first warning for Mr Scheebly. I think things calmed down a little after that.

There were also times in this switchyard I had to get everyone out due to Faulk lightning strikes. The lightening would hit earth arresters and dissipate the charge but would be very dangerous working in the conditions in that High Voltage switchyard. So, weather conditions had to be watched especially coming into the wet season.

THE MOUNT ISA CONNECTION

In that switchyard I did learn something interesting. One of the older fellas excavating soil from the ground showed me what pure uranium looks like. Usually where there is copper there is uranium. It's in the form of a yellow rock which they call yellow cake. This is concentrated in the area we were excavating for the footings of the blast wall.

Northwest Queensland is full of pure high-grade uranium. The only reason they are not able to mine it is because of the *Greenies*. They had a part in closing down a mine called *Mary Kathleen* east of Mount Isa. All that is left of Mary Kathleen is the mining hole now filled with a green-bluish water which you cannot swim in although some silly people do, and the fish are three-eyed. All the buildings from the old community accommodation back down the road are all gone except the remnants of the concrete pads which the buildings were once on.

So in between overseeing or babysitting Mr Scheebly and his crew, I was creating an inventory of switchgear for Stanwell power station at Mount Isa. This power station supplied at the time the power for Mount Isa Mines, the Mount Isa Township and other smaller mines, from gas fired generators, previously coal fired. I would be back at this power station some years later doing switch gear maintenance.

Their electrical equipment was left in a real mess, both in the main store and containers. So, I had the job of itemising every shelf, placing it in order and also organising the containers across the road. When opened, I found that termites had found a new home amongst the brand-new electrical equipment. I was also told to be careful, there might be a few snakes around.

This Kiwi boy had not come across snakes at this point and was taking every precaution not to.

The first thing I did was toss everything out of all three containers early in the morning before the sun came out. By mid-morning, working in the sun would become extremely hot.

Then I decimated the termite mounds, cleaned everything out, then restocked all three containers in orderly fashion. I did this in about two days and then moved into the main store.

I don't understand why people don't place items back properly as a register always records what is in stock.

So I got stuck removing everything shelf-by-shelf. I documented every item in the whole store and sent through to Brisbane. This was my introduction to computerised spreadsheets with every item itemised. This had taken me two weeks, in between working with Mr Scheebly and Co and I couldn't wait to get out of the power station store. Working in an office would actually drive me around the bend if I had to do this full time.

I had worked previously on an underground project for Downer EDI mining, upgrading the control systems for the lead conveyors. That had been a five-week project on level 21 and it would be another good four months on the surface team, installing all the electrical control systems for the number two concentrator ball and sag mills. So, within the two-and-a-half years I worked in Mount Isa, I gained a lot of mining experience and there would be more to come.

There were two other projects I had been called into help with

THE MOUNT ISA CONNECTION

on a Downer EDI mining contract for Xstrata mining. One would be directly under an electrical engineer by the name of Dave. Dave was also a pilot, and we would fly the outbacks together and generally meet up for a meal during the week at the Irish Club to discuss weekend activities. This project would once again be in the number two switchyard where I worked previously with Mr Scheebly and co. This time, I had to reconstruct the overhead switch gear and lines to contain a new transformer bank that would supply a third ball mill for the number two lead concentrator. This was quite a big project as tunnels for underground cables had to be built in concrete structure to the new high voltage substation. The infrastructure had to be built first before heavy cables could laid and transformer installed. I didn't quite get to see the end of this project as the Global Financial Crisis hit halfway through the project and all construction stopped for about six months. I had been asked by Mitch, the engineer at site services who had done the paperwork for all the isolations and power lock out boxes, if I would have been interested in working onsite for Xstrata mining. At the time, my family was in New Zealand and we had just built a new house. This would mean having stay and live in Mount Isa at my own expense, still not being able to go home for weeks at a time. My two girls were in high school and at a private college. This would not have been a good idea having to uproot them at some expense, my wife leaving her job and not knowing what to expect living in remote far North Queensland. Reluctantly, I had to decline the offer. As a result, I would spend the next three months back in New Zealand with no job and no income because of the global financial crisis in 2008. So halfway through I was on my way home. Just prior to leaving on my break, a high voltage substation had completely exploded, taking out the copper concentrator and the underground power on all levels. This had been the result of a trolley circuit breaker, in which the pins are wound up into the contacts. Apparently, the pins on the contact had not been locked in properly and were arcing away till eventually the arcing generated enough current to cause an explosion. And it did big time, like a bomb going off. Instead of having two spare backup transformers, which they could change over to when other transformers needed to be serviced, they had to ring the main transformers in the switchyard with no backups. A new HV substation would have to be built and brought in to replace the badly damaged substation. Xstrata was looking for someone to blame as this was major damage. Fortunately, I had gone home on my break and came back to see this. Eventually, a new substation was brought in and six months later, the transformer and terminations were completed in 2009. I think the ball mill was completed within the same time period.

The other project, I worked with a supervisor by the name Barry on a project installing some PLC control systems in the number two or around the number two lead concentrator.

We had been working in and out of a CO_2 gas high voltage substation. If for any reason there is a fire or an explosion, the CO_2 bottles are discharged automatically, the sensors having picked up smoke.

Before entering these substations, security has to be notified as the CO_2 bottles have to be isolated by a manual isolation switch inside. These substations are locked, and only authorised persons are allowed. However, if working in one of these substations for more than thirty minutes, Queensland fire has to be notified. If one of these CO2 gas bottles goes off and people are in there, they will never make it out. The CO2 discharge suppresses all oxygen as this is one element of the fire triangle that keeps a fire going.

Now Barry and I had finished our work in a substation and were only required to plug in some power extension cords for running portable appliances. So having notified security of our intentions, they advised us if we are going in the substation for five minutes, not to bother calling them. It was already isolated as the fitters were in there already. Because they didn't see us visually advise security, they all got upset. This was a big mistake; these two Xstrata fitters saw us make this move with no security acknowledgement. Two rules, one for contractors and one for Xstrata employees.

These fitters immediately notified the chief electrician of the copper concentrator, and he smartly came down.

"I want to see your JHA (job safety analysis)," he demanded. His next question: "Where on this JHA is your provision for entering a CO2 substation without isolation or security notification?"

Our response was that we followed procedure and security told us if we were only going in for five minutes or less, don't bother calling.

Next question: "Who were the guys?"

Our response: "We don't know as they were a phone call away."

His next: "I want to see your superintendent and manager."

Mike the superintendent and Colin the manager came down. Colin had this stern-looking face and wanted to make a point and so it was me who had to take the fall. This starts to get funny. Having spoken to the copper concentrator chief electrician and asked who gave authorisation of not calling security before entering, we gave the same explanation. "If you're only going in for five minutes or less, don't bother calling us." They asked again who these fellas were and again, we replied, "We don't know. We only spoke with them on the phone prior."

Next thing Colin says, in a stern voice, "I want to see you in the board room right away," so I packed up everything and drove down to the Downer office. I walked into the boardroom. Colin proceeds to tell me, "No, you shouldn't have been in there. I'm going to have to give you two days stand down." I waited for him to finish and told him once again that it was security that advised us to do what we did. Then he said, "Who were these fellas?"

I'm not sure if any of these guys ever listen to me but I gave the same explanation again: "I don't know. I was only on the phone with them, no visual contact."

Next thing every tradesperson is called into the board room, having come off site, and a safety briefing is given. Next thing we all have to do is go and sit through an hour induction with Xstrata safety on entering and leaving a CO_2 substation.

So, Colin gives me supposedly two days stand down. This incident happened Wednesday so on the Thursday with the first day off, Colin rings me and says, in his gruff voice, "I want to see you in the office 7:00 a.m. tomorrow morning." *Good*, I thought, *I am going back to work*. Well, Friday morning came and here I was, sitting in Colin's office. Colin said to me in his gruff voice, "Just had the manager of the copper concentrator on the phone and we have to go down and see him. He is not happy. You are going to have to take everything he gives you."

I said, "Colin, I'm not going to take that. I am going to tell him as it is."

Colin looks at me and says, "Oh no, you're not."

And I say, "Oh yes, I am." Then I said, "Barry the supervisor was there as well." Then Colin says, "Should I give him two days stand down as well?"

"I am not going to dobb Barry in as well," I said.

We drove down to site and proceeded to the concentrator office. Colin came into the manager's office and sat in the corner listening in. I thought it was so funny.

I introduced myself to the manager and then he began to ask me,

THE MOUNT ISA CONNECTION

"How long have you been registered as an electrician?"

"Twenty-five years in New Zealand and five years in Queensland."

He then decided to give me this speech. "We don't like risktakers."

I quietly waited for him to finish and then said, "It was your fellas in security that advised us on procedures." He asked who these fellas were. Colin just about fell out of his chair, and I said, "I don't know. It was a phone call, not a person-to-person interview."

I seemed to have this conversation ten times but I played their game.

Then the manager said, "I'm going to follow up," and then that was end of the conversation. Never heard anything again.

I drove back to the office. Colin never said a word. From the office, I went back to work on another part of the site.

Next day, Barry rings me up, saying, "You want to hear something funny? We went back into that CO2 substation and contacted security about isolation. They said straight out, 'If you're only going in there or less than five minutes, don't bother calling us.'"

> *In school, you're taught a lesson and then given a test.*
> *In life, you're given a test that teaches you a lesson.*
> — TOM BODETT —

I had just about come to the end of my first two-and-a-half years in Mount Isa before the global financial crisis and as I have already said in my previous book, my engineering friend and I would quite often go flying in the Queensland outback when we had some down time. We flew a single engine Cessna 182 between us, covering a number of air nautical miles north towards the gulf, east towards Townsville, and we were on our way to Boulia Camel races when the GFC hit that weekend. Our time off was cancelled and I was booked on a Qantas flight back to New Zealand that Saturday.

I have had some unusual events flying in and out of New Zealand to the Isa. Flying out of Auckland, New Zealand, within twenty minutes a fella walking up the aisle collapsed into my lap and had a bowel movement at the same time. The hosties managed to place an oxygen mask on him and revive him to a conscious state, but I had to go and wash myself.

Another time checking in at Brisbane airport for flight Mount Isa, this smart fella checked me into a seat in business class with another fella with the same name. You know what's going to happen, I turned up first. I'm just getting comfortable and then he rocks up advising me that I am in his seat. Checking our tickets, we had the same name for the one seat. The hostie said one of us had to go and would be placed on the next flight. They all looked at me. Obviously I had drawn the short straw, I would have to get off. But in saying that, my bags were still on the plane, it was about to depart, and they had to get my bags off. For security, you and your bags have to be on the same plane. The plane was delayed by half an hour and I didn't feel too bad after all. What goes round comes round.

Another time, I landed in Brisbane and transferred to the domestic terminal to catch the flight to Mount Isa. Three persons had breached security so the whole of the domestic terminal had to go through security again. There were queues backlogging out to the street. Flights were delayed all over Australia and we didn't get into Isa till late that night.

And this flight leaving on the Saturday when the global financial crisis hit. I was booked on a flight in a seat right down the back in the middle, you guessed it next to a rather large young lady. I apologised to her and asked the steward to put me up in business class as I am a frequent flyer or else I would be suffocated on a three-hour trip across the Tasman.

The crew hemmed and hawed and then quickly placed me in business class where I had everyone waiting on me. That was great, enjoying the comforts and relaxation in larger seats. It would not be the last time I flew business class. Once you have tasted the comforts, you are always somehow wanting to get there again. That's where becoming a Qantas gold or platinum member came in handy as I picked up a lot of points for all my travelling.

Nothing would beat the comforts of a business jet though, which each major company should have. (Some do).

Facing the Global Financial Crisis in New Zealand and Australia

Some people went through this crisis as if nothing happened. Others lost their jobs, their homes, and some their reputation.

For three months, I had no work in New Zealand. The bills were piling up and initially my Australian tax return that year gave me some reprieve. I had just built this lovely new home, coming home to finish all the electrical wiring terminations to power up and have it signed off so we could live in it. The bank always wanted to be paid at the end of every month plus council rates, the power and insurances. These are just the first few necessities with the cost of living. I had two girls we were funding through private schooling and schooling incidental costs on top of that. It was tough and by the end of 2008, I was asked to go back to Australia to work on some commercial building projects in Townsville that had been put on hold during this time. Eventually, I picked up electrical work on the big expansion of Lavarack Barracks, which is Australia's biggest military deployment base. A special security pass was required for all contractors working on base. This expansion continued for a number of years well after I had left. It was local work and I was living in a company house in Townsville. Again, I would be spending time away from Vijaya and the girls to earn and pay for expenses in New Zealand as well as living expenses in Australia.

When people say they are doing it tough, try being away from your family months at a time, sometimes only having twenty dollars in your pocket at the end of the week because you are sending as much as you can home to pay living costs as well as living and cooking for yourself in rented accommodation and then trying to save some to pay for your flight home. This was not the

FACING THE GLOBAL FINANCIAL CRISIS

mines where everything was paid for, including your flights. This was a serious downturn. We are heading now for something even worse in a major world recession as this problem has never been resolved since 2008 and it is now 2022.

The months spent wiring and upgrading buildings on the barracks site helped with finances and running costs at home although for a long time, we were playing catch up.

They had active military personnel on this part of the base and military police were always watching us and monitoring speeds in company vehicles. A ticket issued on base is the same as a civilian ticket and you can actually be kicked off base. Fortunately, we didn't get run over by any tanks or heavy armoured vehicles, which I did see happening on military displays.

Also, at the time, I was living with some very grubby fellas. I don't recommend living in a house with five fellas as you're always going to get the two or three that are clean and the other two, you're always cleaning up after them.

I should have learnt this lesson when working in Christchurch all those years ago and having a nice apartment between four of us. It was me and a little Filipino fella always cleaning up after an English and a South American fella, whose mummies had always cleaned up after them. We would be consistently removing their rubbish, having asked them previously to keep the place clean for inspections.

This work lasted until the end of March 2009 and by then I had applied for work building a jet-fuelled turbine power generator for origin power. The supervisor I had worked with at the Lavarack barracks had got me onto this project. It was run by General Electric, so we had engineers from GE USA, Canada, Singapore, and China. I had this Chinese electrical programmer engineer assigned to me. He was the nicest Chinese fella I have ever met.

He called himself Henry as his real name was hard to pronounce. He would come with me everywhere. He was just a little fella, but

he would come out with me after work for meals, on weekend road trips, church activities and flying. Yes, I gave him a flight in a light aircraft. He filmed every shop, inside every church service, from the air, from the ground and I know he wasn't a spy as he wanted to get his wife and child out of China. Henry didn't like how they paid him on a Chinese salary compared to his colleagues from other countries. Henry didn't like some of the countries they sent him to especially Saudi Arabia. "Too hot hot, I no go back." Henry told me of his upbringing and family's expectations and he didn't want that for his children. Henry had a compassionate heart. He wanted to bring his family to Australia. This was 2009 and it's now 2022.

I never saw Henry in person again after the turbine project. But I did keep in email contact for a couple of years.

On construction of the turbine generator, we piped out all the pressure tubing, installed pressure instruments, power systems cables, PLC cables to all the panels for the new programmes and for the engineers to design the programmes.

I met up with two other fellas, Lincoln Johnson, instrument technician, and Kerry Wood House, a boiler maker. These fellas have been my close friends for the last ten years. We have worked together, travelled together, helped each other together and we support each other. These are just a few of the network of friends we established from all over Australia from different projects to mine sites. We may not see each other for a while but we still keep in contact.

The turbine project went on for over a year whilst I was there, and new tower high voltage lines had to be built into the incoming feeder network.

The whole idea of this project was to boost the power supply when demand is high in the summertime due to heavy usage of power in the Townsville area due to high temperatures and necessary cooling systems. Because this is an expensive operation, turbine is not run consistently.

It was interesting to watch the new lines being strung with the use of a helicopter and elevated work platforms, working across the main highway south of Townsville with big arms to prevent lines falling onto the road.

The helicopter would bring one line across at a time and the helicopter would be holding that line at about a 60-degree angle. The fellas on the elevated work platform would clamp the lines from the helicopter and chain block them up to the top of tower insulators. The helicopter would go back and get another line and the lowering to the elevated work platform claps would be the same until all six lines were securely clamped to insulators on top of towers. We watched them work these lines from the top of turbine platform on a reasonably windy day.

This was a clean project too and probably the last I did in Townsville. Most of my other work there is maintenance at the Zinc Refinery (Sun Metals) and a little maintenance at the solar farm for Sun Metals.

All the engineers at the power station commissioned the whole system and we did get to see it running on a short time basis. I think

starting and stopping during the commissioning would have burnt up more jet fuel in the turbine than having it properly running. The level in the big fuel tank could be seen dropping.

It really was just a jet engine on the ground.

Now there was another South African fella that worked with us. His name was Don Kraut, and he was always on the lookout for a bargain. When the job was finishing, he approached Layton Construction management to relieve them of all the big drums of cable and negotiated a ridiculous price for all the drums. Don brought in a heavy vehicle, had all the drums lifted on by forklift, chained them all on and drove home. Some of those drums were full drums. I know he sold them off at full price and made 100% profit. That was Don, always on the lookout for a bargain.

Don would eventually work over in Papua New Guinea with a company and take over appliances, selling them to locals on the side.

The world was still pulling itself out of the global financial crisis and we were finishing projects that had to be finished. Once they were finished, work became a bit scattered and I remember by the end of 2009 having not worked for a month or so before Christmas. I did not have enough money to go back to New Zealand for Christmas with Vijaya and the girls. That was a very lonely Christmas.

I had paid for Rachel and Cilla to fly over and spend some time with me in our apartment in Townsville during their school holidays that year. At that time, I had just finished at the Origin Power Station, thinking the next project was just around the corner. The little apartment I had just bought about six months before had seemed a better option at the time rather than living with a few dirty smelly fellas and having Rachel and Cilla stay here would be more convenient.

So, Rachel and Cilla came. It was their first trip to Townsville as a year and a half previous they had both come with my mother to Mount Isa when I couldn't get home.

We would spend time at friends' places at the beaches up north of Townsville and spend some time on Magnetic Island, jet skiing around the bays.

We would also spend ten days of driving around North Queensland and going to some fun places for dinners and lunches. I had a good time with them.

In that time, we also had a very special friend, a retired minister from the Salvation Army of New Zealand who made the effort to come and see me. It was good timing as my two girls were there as well. Cole O'Dywer had been a family friend in New Zealand and liked an adventure. He liked training. I think Townsville had an interesting starting point for trains. Trains coming into Townsville were the passenger trains, the mining trains from Northwest Queensland, the acid trains out to phosphate mine, and the freight trains that came in to Townsville, no commuter trains though. Part of his Australian experience was to catch one train during each trip through different states or territories. On his way back down to South Queensland, he would catch the tilt train from Townsville to Brisbane.

Cole also came on our little excursion trip to Magnetic Island, which is a twenty-minute ferry ride from Townsville Port. We would drive around that island spending time in the warm waters of the different beaches avoiding all the stingers (Box Jelly Fish) and having fun on jet skis.

Since living in Queensland for the last fourteen years, we have experienced the Barrier Reef, hiking down some of the great rivers, avoiding the crocodiles of Queensland, camped up in the lake areas of the Tablelands where temperatures are a lovely few degrees cooler. We have flown and tripped around the state, including a number of cattle stations that spanned kms. It's a very big area.

Rachel and Cilla did go home after the ten days. They left me a lovely card saying they had had a lovely time. I didn't really want to see them go but knew Vijaya, Rachel, Cilla were coming over to join me in January 2010.

The Mount Gordon Mine Start Up

*If you are not having fun,
you are doing something wrong.*
—GROUCHO MARX—

Vijaya and the girls had just arrived in early January 2010. I had prepared for their coming, setting up everything in our little unit on the waterfront in Townsville.

We had enrolled Cilla for her last two years at Anadale Christian College. Rachel went looking for work and Vijaya was applying for work as a preschool teacher.

In 2010, the Australian economy was just starting to kick off again. Mining of resources was coming out of the doldrums and I was able to pick up a two-week on one-week off roster at Burla Mount Gorden Mine, Northwest Queensland. This mine is 125 km north of Mount Isa, a copper mine.

We would fly into Mount Isa and bus the 125 km to Mount Gordon. At the camp, we were assigned our rooms. Depending whether we were on night shift or day shift, we have breakfast at the diner 5:30 a.m. or 5:30 p.m. and prepare to bus onsite leaving at 5:30 a.m. for day shifts or 5:30 p.m. for night shifts. Our actual  shift started at 6:00 a.m. and ended at 6:00 p.m. days and vice versa nights.

This mine had just been taken out of care of maintenance as the copper concentrate prices had started to increase once again. As electricians onsite, we were recommissioning ball mills, conveyors, electric motor, VSD (variable speed drives) substations, switchboard rooms, process instrumentation, mill water pontoon motors on the lake.

The mine was processing high grade copper concentrate from underground. The underground decline was only about 500 meters deep then. I remember being called to do a quick underground induction.

The power from the main incoming feeder had gone off from Mount Isa and all the under power dropped out. There was no one down there at the time but the water was starting to back up without the submersible pumps running. Usually if light vehicles, heavy machinery and personnel are down underground when the power goes off, vehicles and personnel must get up to the surface quickly as the ventilation fans have stopped and diesel fumes become a problem.

When the power did come back on, the fitter and I went down to check the ventilation motors, the sump pump motors had to be turned back on all the way down the decline and the radio repeater stations had to be reset all the way down as well.

We were down there for about two hours, making sure everything was working. The mine had had massive flooding in the last wet season and this year there had been quite a bit of rain. The water levels around the mine were starting to build up and stop banks were installed in preparation for a heavy deluge of water. Surface generators were pumping water into the tailings dams up top. Prior to the heavy rain in the last two years, the lake where the water is pumped to the mine was bone dry. Cattle had been seen walking across the lake. Freshwater crocs were on the other side with little water. When the monsoon rains did come, the lake was full once again.

THE MOUNT GORDON MINE START UP

One night, one of the mine's main water pumps dropped out. So, the fitter and I had to take a motorised dinghy in the dark with a torch to the pontoon platform where the electric motors sit. Don't forget there are freshwater crocs there in the dark.

We primed the dead motor, started it up again, boated back and drove back to the mine. The water levels were rising, and then the motor failed again. So, we had to drive back out to the lake, launch the dinghy, motor back out to the pontoon and prime it all again. We did this five times before we decided to bring the standby pump on. We disconnected the failed motor and connected the standby motor, thinking it was all good to go. What we didn't do was Megger test the insulation on the windings. We powered the standby motor up and it went BOOM and blew the isolator switch for the motor up. So, we still only had one pump motor working and one motor down and with no spare and isolator switch that had blown up.

Getting parts out to the mine would take a few days. I had to write a report in the morning to say the standby pump had failed due to water contamination.

Night shift had its benefits because there is usually no management around, and you are given the preventative maintenance check sheets to do for the night on the plant. When they are done, we entertain ourselves.

A fella by the name of Phil Bannano rocks up onsite. I have worked with Phil before, a funny fella. We called him the banana man with a high pitched voice.

Now Phil decided to look up his family history on the internet. He got a surprise when he found out the Bannano name was associated with Mafia hierarchy. I think he quickly closed the file.

The chief sparky Peter Hytch was very good with all his staff and made sure we knew what was required of us to keep the plant up and running. We all had hard rock mining backgrounds and most plants are very similar.

We had another tall fella called Max. Max was a Papua New Guinean national with a big smile on his face. We would walk and talk as we did field checks on the outer areas of the mine. With the heavy rain, the tailing dams were filling up quite fast as well as underground pumps pumping, gen sets all pumping water into the tailings. We had the job of making sure the electrical pumps were all working.

Max had come off a high voltage power station. He lived at the time in Mount Isa. The Isa is a hub to George Fisher, 20 km from Mount Isa, Ernest Henry out of a place called Cloncurry, Lady Annie next to Mount Gordon, Phosphate Hill roughly two hours south of Mount Isa and Century Mine, six hours north of Mount Isa. All essential freight passes through Mount Isa to be transported to these sites. Mount Isa is also the hub for cattle stations in the area. Many of the stations have their own aircraft and fly in to get supplies and equipment as well as using heavy haulage for bigger installations going to these cattle stations.

I remember a few years later IPL (Incitec Pivot), which is an international company that owns Phosphate Hill Mine, also ran the Acid Plant at Mount Isa Mines. This day it had a broken part that urgently needed replacing. This part had to be especially flown in from Europe. So early one Sunday morning whilst lying in bed at the Isa, this massive Russian Antonov aircraft flies from the south over us into the Mount Isa airport with the urgent part for the acid plant, engines roaring.

That's Mount Isa, where all freight is delivered to or from.

Mount Gordon Mine was up and running again and we can say all of our team had an input in helping to get it up and running over those early months. Copper concentrate was being shipped out once again to the Port of Townsville by the Indian owners.

There were two other things at Mount Gordon. First, there was

THE MOUNT GORDON MINE START UP

an operator who had a medical condition. Every time he sneezed, he farted, and this could go on for a while. I burst out laughing. He told me it wasn't a laughing matter, it was a medical condition. Had to bite my lip.

Second, cane toads came out in droves everywhere. If you had a golf club, they were good for practicing. These things are big, ugly, and poisonous. They have a coating they excrete on their backs, which is harmful to any predator. They seem to love bright lights as well as water.

The company eventually bought their own charter aircraft, which flew directly into the Burla Mount Gordon Airstrip. We were flown out from there when our shift was finished.

Another reason most remote mines have their own airports is that the Royal Flying Doctor Service might need to airlift critically injured patients.

All up we spent from January till end of April onsite here at Mount Gordon.

With the process of producing copper concentrate in its pure state, it is mined first as rock, then transported to the surface by mining vehicles. Places like Mount Isa Mines and many others have an underground jaw crusher or cone crushers. From the underground crushers, the ore body is usually transported to the surface by conveyors to the ball and sag mills. The ball mill has steel balls dumped into the chamber and as the mill spins with water added, it crushes the ore down into a softer mass. The sag mill is used to grind large pieces into small pieces. From there, it goes through the floatation tanks, which are big ponds with a big arm moving clockwise around the tank. From the arm are either suspended chains or steel bracing, which takes out all the impurities and causes them to drop to the bottom of the tank. From there the remanence is piped through to the floatation tanks and mixed with chemicals. In these big floatation tanks, the copper through the interaction of the chemicals is pushed to the surface over the sides. Also inside the tanks are big agitators, which stirs the process up.

From here the copper is dried into its raw state as copper concentrate. There are a few other little processes in between but this gives you a general idea of the process of copper. Processing lead or zinc is similar. Coking coal, iron ore and gold are completely different. With the concentrate at Mount Isa Mines, they have copper and lead smelters and they are able to process the concentrates in tablets and lead ingots. The copper tablets are further refined into pure sheets of copper at the Townsville Copper refinery through electrolysis.

Zinc Production at Century Mine

Common sense is like deodorant.
The people who need it never use it.

From 2010 till late 2011, I was trained to work on the electrics of Komatsu 830e, Komatsu 630e, etc, diggers and loaders. The Komatsu 830e carried 200 tonnes of zinc rock and the Komatsu 630e carried just over 100 tonnes. These trucks have electric wheel motors which are used as the main breaking for the loads these trucks carry. The mechanics of the trucks in motion drive a three-phase ac alternator. The leads from the alternator are connected to rectifier behind the truck cab. The rectifier converts ac to dc, alternating current to direct current. This powers up a dc board near the driver's cab with 24vdc. This is really the brain of the truck. From here, field contacts can be energised for breaking and power systems bringing the resistor bank in motion or what they called the retard system, which can be set at required kms per hour for electric breaking to come down a decline down the haul access road. The retard switch is usually never set above 30 kms per hour as a speed like this is very dangerous with a load of 200 tonnes coming down a haul road.

The static system is the brain of the truck, a little white box with dc components and 24v battery to govern certain systems on truck. A laptop can be plugged here or with an internal laptop connection behind the driver's seat, and then you can download every event in real time for the day. This includes loads, weight balances, faults which can occur and we are called out in the field to fix, overbearing temperatures in wheel motors, and general internal breakdowns in the operator cab.

The haul trucks came in for 150, 250, 500, 1000, 2000 hour services. These are schedule maintenance times and the greater hours, the bigger the overhaul and inspections, especially on the wheel motors. They check for any wear and that the shape hasn't worn down from its symmetrical shape and also not pitted from worn brushes that could have caused flash overs.

I could go on in detail with checking brushes in alternators and other incidentals but working on these trucks and driving them in for maintenance was fun. One of the best jobs I had.

My work colleague on my shift was big Dave, lovely man, a bit younger than me and very respected. I learnt a lot from him as he had been working in the heavy maintenance workshop at Century for some time. The contractor I was working under, Phil, who owned the company Haulpac, was a very good and challenging boss. I think he scratched his head a few times at my antics and fun behaviour, but he was a very respected operator and friend.

There were other fellows I worked with that left not long after I had started. They too were great guys to work with and I would again work with them in later years.

We had a Toyota Land Cruiser V8 for us electricians and fitters. Working around heavy vehicles and heavy plant machinery, you had to be always in radio contact, as these big machines had blind spots. Also we had to keep a required distance of around 50 meters when driving behind them in case of roll back.

The haul trucks had big Komatsu, Cummins or Detroit engines and driving them, you had only forward and reverse. One of these trucks new is worth around $2,000,000 apiece. These trucks run 24/7 on two shifts on one swing and two shifts on the other, 8/6 nights and 7/7 days, both male and female operators. You have the diggers and escalators in the pit, the blast areas were drilled by drilling rigs all day and night and areas would be barricaded off at certain times by the destination and explosive team so the pit would close when blasting was taking place. There was a designated viewing platform at the top of the pit near the control

room so you could actually see the blasting take place.

Every shift change, we would be taken by bus around and down the pit to observe any changes, road closures or new areas of the pit to become familiar with.

I remember on nights trying to orientate myself around the pit in the dark as you could be called out at any minute for a breakdown.

One night a fella had a stroke in a haul truck and was driving round and round in circles. Another operator and person had to drive up alongside him, jump in the truck and bring the truck to a standstill. Fortunately, the haul truck was on the rom pad where they dump the ore before the crusher and not the haul access road, which would have been a disaster.

The fella was flown out and hospitalised for a time and did recover to eventually come back to work but I don't think it was driving again.

On a breakdown in one of the haul trucks one night, a woman driver complained she kept losing her electric braking. I jumped in the truck with her, plugged in the laptop and drove down the haul road, watching the electric braking system on the laptop. We lost

ZINC PRODUCTION AT CENTURY MINE

the electric braking. It dropped out as we were going down the haul road. The truck was speeding up. We were looking for a truck pad we could quickly turn onto. Fortunately, the retardant came on prior to turning onto the pad. We parked the haul truck up on the V drain, which is a dip where they park the front wheels of the haul trucks. We shut down the engine and had a quick look inside the resistor bank, which governs the electric braking through the field contractors. We could smell some burning and when we investigated, one of the resistor banks had burnt out. We placed an out of service tag in the cab. This was a job for day shift to isolate interconnecting cables and remove resistor pad, replacing with a new pad.

I would team up with Dave most days and one day it had been raining really hard. Usually haul trucks are parked up as they have no traction on their tyres, they would slide otherwise. A Komatsu 830e had broken down prior to raining and when we got to the shale dumping area, I had to drive the truck back to the workshop. As I began to move the truck off the pad, the back end began fishtailing, moving sideways left to right. I managed to get onto the haul road and then it held some of its traction as the road is hard metal and always being graded. Dave was following 50 meters behind in

the breakdown ute. Heavy vehicles are fixed onsite there and then. If the vehicle needs further attention, it is taken back to the heavy vehicle workshop.

Like anything else onsite, every piece of equipment or heavy machinery, you have to be authorised to drive or operate. We in the heavy workshop were all passed out on driving everything except loaders and excavators. The fellow who passed us out on heavy machinery, they called him Snooze. Every morning in the pass meeting, he would fall asleep and snore, he wasn't that old either. Our pass meetings give the day's maintenance plan and handovers from the previous shift. Any safety issues are brought up as well as any incidents that may have occurred the previous night.

Well, Snooze came with me this day as I drove down and around the pit. I can tell you, if you are not driving and sitting in the passenger's seat, the movements and the loud noise easily puts you to sleep. I've been there when I had to do two hours with the operator driver for pit orientation.

Well, this day Snooze was on the tip of falling asleep in the cab, so I thought, *I have got to show him as part of the pass out to do a reverse dump with the tray up,* purposely stopping on the shale area all of a sudden and extending the tray in the up position. He fell forward in his seat with the seatbelt on and then back. He woke up in a hang of a hurry. He passed me out very quickly, not saying much more after that.

We were in the workshop one day and one of the fitters on our shift brought back a haul truck for maintenance. Now the procedure when you start up a Komatsu haul truck or any heavy equipment is to give one blast on the horn for start-up, two blasts of the horn to move forward, and three blasts of the horn to reverse. Now when you reverse, you always have a spotter on the driver's side. He can see you from his mirror and you can direct him to avoid any obstructions. The right side of the truck is a blind spot, the driver cannot see much from that side.

Now on this day, the fitter did not realise the tray was still a quarter full of ore. When the fitters bring and park haul trucks in the workshop, the first thing they do is to lift the tray to full extension. Well, this old mate lifted the tray to full extension and dumped half a tray of ore on the workshop floor. He had to get it cleaned up. He didn't think it was funny, but we did.

Then there was big Norm, a fitter who loved to sing. He wasn't bad either. Nights were his best performances as there was a few electricians and fitters around.

Norm would introduce us to us to his world of music, which incorporated a wide range of songs. He also introduced me to bringing out my full complements of music. So, bringing out a funnel, piece of hose and my mouthpiece, I began playing a concerto on the top of a haul truck one night. The fellas took full film footage of me with my helmet on, standing on the top of the truck, playing this piece of entertaining music on a bit of hose pipe and a funnel. They thought it was hilarious.

I'm not sure if it went viral, as management wouldn't have been too pleased if anyone had seen it.

Some of the best times I had on any site were with these fellas. We worked together, we laughed together, we helped each other on the whole crew.

Then there was Phil B and his off-sider Milton. Phil had this frozen smile. You didn't know if he was laughing at you or laughing at himself, but he was good to work with and he knew his stuff.

We quite often gave these fellas a hand on nights if they needed it and they would do the same for us. As long as we got the maintenance done, management was happy.

Now every pass meeting, the room would be full of maintenance and office staff. Everyone had a turn in doing the presentation of jobs for today, reporting of incidents or incidents free from the following day or night, what could be done better.

Well, we had come back on shift after Cyclone Yasi, which had been one of the most devastating cyclones to hit far North Queensland in 2011. It was very wet and the rain bands from the cyclone had travelled roughly 1000 km inland and we were still getting the effects of this the week we went back to work. Flying in that day, the mining charter had to abort a landing at Lawn Hill airport and fly back to Townsville due to weather. An extra flight was later made to take our crew out for night shift. This time both aircraft were able to land.

On night shift, I had been checking all the workshops, ensuring adequate electrical protection when I came across the boiler maker workshop and found they had all their electrical extension power leads on the workshop floor. My first reaction: "Fellas, these leads should not be in the water. Hang them up or someone is going to get a real belt." As I shifted them, I got a real belt of 230v.

Big Norm told me I must go and report this and be checked. I'm not sure if this was the best thing to do, except from a medical point of view. I had to go and have an ECG and a medical check-up. They even had to go and replace all the safety protection for electrical power circuits on all the MCC boards. Then the paperwork came. I had to fill in a report. Then came the pass meeting as I mentioned above. They called me the "Shock Absorber" and I had to do a full presentation in the meeting about the dangers of water and power. "Not a good combination." Well, you guessed it, Dr Phil or Phil B and Milton could not contain themselves. I think a few others were in fits of laughter too. I didn't mind but the new supervisor who had come to our department hated doing paperwork and I think this was the beginning of my downfall at Century Mine, although management and the mines manager wanted me around.

I probably educated a few boiler makers especially as well as others willing to listen after their fits of laughter about the dangers of water and electrical energy. "They don't work well together."

ZINC PRODUCTION AT CENTURY MINE

This wouldn't be the last amusement I would have on these fitters and electrical staff.

There would be times when we would have to do running checks on haul trucks that had been stood down to keep the engine hours down. MMG, the mining company, had a hold down yard. A number of these haul trucks were kept here for a time till they were required. Over the other side of the lay down is a graveyard of haul trucks taken out of service. Parts were quite often robbed when needed urgently. So, every week one of us would drive each of these haul trucks around the top of the pit to keep the hydraulic oil in circulation.

It was on a day I was doing some running checks on a Komatsu 830e with the fitters to bring two of these trucks back on online. The operators had left the haul truck I was driving out of diesel. Now these haul trucks take something like 4000 litres of diesel and within two twenty-four-hour shifts, they burn this amount of diesel off. What I should have done was gotten the fuel cart up to fill the diesel tank up. Instead, I decided to drive the haul truck down to the fuel bay where a fuel person would fill the tank up. Remember, this a 200-tonne truck. The fitters had just gone back to the workshop. I started to drive this thing down the haul road. I had the tyre fitters behind me, at the same time keeping their 50-meter distance. The haul truck operators had complained that the haul access road had too much water dumped by the water cart to keep the dust levels down. Not realising this, I came down that haul road with the electric brake motor retard switch set to 25 km per hour. The wheel motors had come on at this point. This caused the back end of the haul truck to slide ninety degrees to face the windrow (the

bank). I had no option but to just let it go. The tyre fellas were behind me and saw what had happened. Quickly radioing my situation and what had happened, I proceeded to get the truck off the access road and to the fuel bay.

The fitters had heard the call over the radio and when they heard it was me, they were laughing their heads off and couldn't get back there quick enough. I didn't panic, I just had to let it take its course. What I did have to do was fill in a report. There was no drug and alcohol test required as the haul truck operators had complained about the conditions. Speaking to one of my operator friends later, he told me that he had actually spun 180 degrees once on a very wet haul road.

Once again, the MMG supervisor had to get out of his comfort zone and write a report. He was shaking his head. My boss Phil told me I had done the right thing. In his office he had another fella Trent who monitored all the truck movements and speed by GPS trackers that were on every haul truck.

That was another strike, strike two by the MMG supervisor. What these haul truck operators couldn't get away with was that each truck was being monitored and their excuse for excess speeds or inappropriate breakdowns they would radio up about.

At the workshop nothing was said as no damage was done and no one was hurt. Everyone was asking, "Are you alright? Do you have any anxiety?" I could have lived that up, but it would have been extremely funny. I just shrugged my shoulders and said, "Put it down to a learning curve." It was brought up in the pass meeting next morning and I did give a good explanation. But as usual, I got a few good laughs trying to keep a straight face.

Actually, when I did leave, I really missed some of those fellas I worked with.

We as breakdown service electricians had pit passes so we were required to be on call for breakdowns on the bottom of the pit face day and night. Lighting towers were placed at essential parts of the pit, on access and haul roads, literally where heavy machinery was required to operate.

These lighting towers came on at certain times to bring the pit to life at night. My off sider Big Dave had actually designed a sequence for these lighting towers to come on automatically at dusk. These were part of our maintenance schedule. Big Dave was quite a smart fella and I hope he gets to read my story, knowing I really appreciated working with him and another fella called Roger for the time I was at Century Mine in Northwest Queensland.

Most of all the crews flew in from Cairns or Townsville. Alliance was the mining charter aircraft and there would be a flight into the mine on Mondays, bringing management in, and out on Thursdays or Fridays for management to leave. For maintenance we were out every Wednesday. Our roster was 8/6 days, 7/7 nights.

It was on one of my day shift swings that the night shift crew passed on a job from the hard basket for me. There had been two caravans especially designed for the mine at some considerable cost taken down to a flat area near the bottom of the pit for the operators' crib rooms. These caravans weren't anything special and I really think MMG got ripped off for buying them at an exorbitant price.

However, there were two diesel generators to power up these two caravans with overhead cables running from generators to Caravans. The problem was the generators had to be earthed with an earth stakes in the ground. Rock, not dirt. Hard rock and a copper stake don't go together very well. The other crew thought it was too hard for them. Big Dave's and Richard's crew didn't think it was too tough. What we did was disconnect the power cables, then one of the lady operators we knew drove a grader to pull the caravans out one at a time. I called up one of my drilling mates to come up from the pit. He chug-chugged up, drilled a 40 mm 2 diameter hole in the rock for both earth pegs. I put the earth pegs in the rock and compacted them. The driller chug-chugged back down to the pit. The operator in the grader pushed the caravans back. We connected the leads back to the generator and caravan, connected up the earth stakes, job done. Night shift came in that night wanting to know how we had done it. No problem. "Come on, tell us how you did it."

"We didn't use an auger bit, we got a drilling rig and a grader, using the combination."

"What, you took a drilling rig out of production?"

"Yep, sure did."

They just laughed their heads off. But the job was done.

Being down in the pit and working with all the operators, you got to know them pretty well. The women operators were the most careful operators and fewer incidents occurred with them.

With heavy vehicles, there are a number of blind spots and radio communications were the priority. We operated on three channels. You cannot pass a haul truck whilst it is moving and when it is stationary, you must make contact with an operator before to get clearance to pass. Loaders and graders would give you an acknowledgement when it was ok to pass. We also had an emergency channel which was monitored all the time and it wasn't till just recently when going back to Century Mine after eight years on another contract that I got to replace batteries for the emergency hut and actually see where it was located. It was a fair distance away on a very high point and four-wheel drive only access.

With haul trucks and many other mobile plants, the batteries are located right up top. With the haul trucks, right hand side of the top deck. Four 24v batteries. As you can imagine, a lot of current is needed to turn over those big Cummins engines. On a few occasions, it wasn't unusual to have to jump start from the break down ute battery power pack for these trucks. Usually, operators left electrical equipment running and their stereos, which were turned up so loud. You would go to start these trucks and just about get blasted out the door. Turning the volume down was

a no-no, especially if you left the job and didn't turn the volume back up.

Dragging these leads all the way to the top deck was an effort and I learnt to jump start the engines eventually from the starter motors underneath the trucks.

One night, going to jump start a haul truck, I accidentally dropped a ring scanner across the terminals of a battery. There was a bit of a flash and when I looked at the end of my ring spanner, I didn't quite recognise the end of it. Big Rodger had a bit of a laugh.

There was another occasion when I was called to jump start a haul truck sitting all by itself at the west Go Line. You had the South Go Line and the West Go Line. These are where the operators park their trucks up in the V drain before going to Crib or Lunch breaks. One night on shift, I went to jump start this truck from underneath the starter motor. Everything was going good. I had my cap lamp on in the dark and had dragged the long jumper leads under the truck, clipping them onto the starter motor. What I didn't realise was that I had clipped them round the wrong way. As I jumped up to the operator's cab and tried to turn over the engine, the dash lights kept flashing on and off. I couldn't understand why I could smell smoke. I quickly raced down the ladder to underneath the truck and found a small fire had started. Racing to put the fire out, which I did, I found I had completely blown the ends off the alligator clips, and they were big clips. Fortunately, I hadn't blown anything up on the electronics.

I raced back to the workshop, cut the burnt-out alligator clips off, connected new ones on, then raced back to clean up the blackened starter motor. I jump-started it again and left it there, ready for service.

I never told anyone about this. Everyone would have laughed except management.

> As you get older, three things happen.
> The first is that your memory goes and
> I can't remember the other two.
> —SIR NORMAN WISDOM—

Century mine had a good atmosphere. Big Dave decided to play a trick on two supervisors one night. Whilst they went out for lunch, he swapped the mouses on their computers around so the opposite desk supervisor was spinning the cursor on the other supervisor's desk. They were scratching their heads, wondering what was going on. Big Dave and I were outside, laughing our heads off till they saw us and realised what had happened.

Being able to have a week off in between swings gave me the opportunity to develop some aerial photography for some of the clients I had worked for previously and also help in emergency relief. I remember lying in my room one night at Century Camp, watching the news about a massive earthquake that had rocked Christchurch, New Zealand. I had never ever known Christchurch to have earthquakes as I had lived in the North Island of New Zealand and had experienced plenty of quakes and aftershocks growing up. But in Christchurch, I couldn't believe what I saw. The CBD, the outer part of the city, the port hills, and Lyttleton Harbour were all smashed. My week off was coming and I immediately offered my services to the Salvation Army as I am associated with the Salvation Army church, both in New Zealand and Australia. I told my wife Vijaya and she suggested when I flew back to Townsville on the mining charter, I should immediately take up the Salvos' offer and fly to New Zealand.

The Salvation Army was getting as many volunteers as possible. There were a number of us that flew in from Australia at different times to relieve others.

On arriving we were set up in a special area of a caravan park. Many people had also taken the opportunity to drive into areas of Christchurch that were accessible.

Every night we felt the aftershocks. The first day we were taken to Sydenham on the east side of Christchurch, bypassing the city. We were briefed about going into houses, taking in food and necessary supplies for people, and advised to listen to very scared people. We were given emergency vehicles for each group. Another fella and I had an emergency Land Rover and did we do some kms going into house after house. Driving through the suburbs, with shop faces completely demolished and old buildings completely collapsed, even new housing concrete slap floors broken in half and the liquefaction coming up through the floors, we heard the stories of people escaping buildings in the CBD and those who weren't so fortunate. We went into a house of an old couple who had lost their overseas home that day and were grieving. We had a cup of tea with them and just listened.

Street after street was broken. Day in and day out for around ten days, we were sure we could help. To say people were not ok was an understatement. To show people we cared was what they needed.

I was one of many there only for a short time. These people had to rebuild their lives and their shattered homes. Many left because they couldn't rebuild or didn't want to rebuild. But what I did see was the human spirit and the kindness of many people and businesses, many people joining in prayer not only for Christchurch and its victims but for the presence of God to touch again this city.

Within that ten days, I caught up with many friends and my relatives down in the heart of the South Island of New Zealand. I will always remember the night the Salvos flew me out of Christchurch. A number of the personnel associated with helping the Salvation Army were taking out pieces of bricks as souvenirs. So, I decided to call them Brick Heads, Block Busters, Chip Off the Old Block. They had a great laugh. I'm reminded that bringing joy to people's hearts is priceless

That was my Christchurch effort in my time off from Century Mine.

I'm quite often reminded by those who have always been in a permanent job (no job is permanent and is an archaic way of looking at things) that feeling secure just means not really taking a risk. Sure, sometimes we might struggle but the opportunities come along if you are willing to take them. The people you meet along with life's experiences build your character. Also, you can change lives for the good. I believe this is God's way of helping us connect to him through his word and the way we live. I have my flaws and being away from home can be very lonely. My family doesn't always understand but their needs are met.

At Century Mine, the people I worked with, even a superintendent Peter Tipihi, a fellow countrymen and the mines manager Karl Spelack, I had great respect for. To leave under circumstances from my own management which I didn't care for, these fellas and my shift team didn't want me to go. Or maybe they did. Ha-ha.

It would be another eight years before I would be back at Century Mine. This time, I came under another company, the pit closed, the heavy vehicle workshop, machinery and all personnel gone.

The Lucinda Port Insurance Assessment

I came from Century Mine to do some contracting months after Cyclone Yasi near the end of 2011. Yasi = devastated North Queensland. It demolished everything in its path including the sugar port.

One of the contracts was to assess the electrical damage for the insurance company at the Lucinda sugar port, one-and-a-half hours north of Townsville. The flooring on the main conveyor from shore to port had been ripped out by the heavy winds. On the jetty itself, 11-meter waves had broken some of the concrete fabrication. Also the waves had pummelled their way through the ship loaders and generators, and had taken out two 5-tonne transformers and bowled over a concrete building.

The roadway out to the port from shore was 6 km. One of the longest ports in the Southern Hemisphere and my TA (Trade Assistance) and I were asked to test all the electrics including circuit boards, conveyor pull cords, lighting, and everything else that had power running to it.

We started from shore and worked our way up the tunnel, remembering the floorboards had been ripped out. So we were walking on planks and walking across the steel struts for 6 kms. The ocean was below us and so were some big fish. When we got to the top, we had to come back down and walk the 6 km back to test all the low voltage equipment (12v). These were mainly the wiring to the anodes, which are suspended in the water near the steel columns. These anodes release a 12v charge to neutralise the salt in the water around the columns to reduce the corrosion.

Once the main conveyor was documented and we had finished the testing, we had to assess all the damage on the port.

Some of the main concrete infrastructure at the port had been demolished and sunk. A special diving team and barge had to float the infrastructure up to the surface and repair the damaged berth.

The ship loader substation had salt water right through all the electrics. We had to test all insulation resistance and earthing, and visually check the actual water damage. It was not a pretty sight. We had pages of documented reports for the insurance company. It was a good two-and-a-half weeks checking every electrical component that made up the loading facilities at the port. Initially, there were $50,000,000 in damages.

The high voltage substation was documented as completely damaged. The power was isolated on shore by the sugar mill HV electricians knowing the cyclone was coming a day before. No ships had been berthed in that time due to the storm coming.

What was interesting around that port were the massive fish. It was a fisherman's haven, although there was an exclusion zone for anglers due to the damaged port. My TA did bring his collapsible fishing rod in his bag one day, put a lure on the end of the

THE LUCINDA PORT INSURANCE ASSESSMENT

line and threw it in the water. No sooner had he thrown it in the water than the line whistled away with something very big and snapped. Goodbye, lure. You weren't really allowed to fish off wharf anyway.

Most nights we stayed at the hotel up there at Lucinda but every three or four nights, I would catch a ride with one of the sugar trucks driving back to Townsville Port. I lived within walking distance of the port.

As Lucinda Port was closed to shipping access, the sugar processed from the sugar mills in the area was trucked through and shipped out of Townsville. These road trains, which can be three trailers long, were going 24/7 between Lucinda and the port. In Queensland, because of the huge distances, road trains predominate. It is not unusual to see cattle, mining and container road trains driving throughout Queensland and the Northern Territory.

One of these fellas I had gotten a lift with would be driving between Queensland and Western Australia. And he would do it with short rest breaks and two logbooks. Very risky on health and if he got picked up by the boys in blue, he could have been in a spot of bother. Distance between coast to coast is just over 4000 km one way.

Anyways, this work filled in nicely before I was asked to help with building the electric construction in high voltage switchyards in Central Queensland. The purpose being for the electrics to the coal trains as the mining companies were expanding coal production and larger quantities were needed to be shipped out to the coal ports. To do this, new switchyards had to be built to cope with the high voltage that was required for the electrification of the increase in coal trains. After working in these switchyards, I would be changing over to maintenance in the coal fields.

As I said, the damage done by Cyclone Yasi in 2011 was considerable. The port was rebuilt within a year and ships were able to access their berths at Lucinda Port once again.

Cyclones are very unpredictable. Living in the tropics, you have to be prepared for certain times of the year. The seasons are usually between October and (not till) April with temperatures increasing above 29 degrees Celsius, a lot of moisture being sucked up into the atmosphere and barometric pressure decreasing. The low pressure draws in the warm air. They move in a westerly direction but they can change course very quickly. Once reaching landfall, the power of a cyclone usually diminishes as it needs to consistently pick up moisture, which it cannot on land.

Cyclone Yasi and Cyclone Larry did considerable damage to properties, businesses and farming in those years. In the last twelve years, I have helped clean up many other areas on the coast with Tropical Cyclones passing through.

> *"If you find it hard to laugh at yourself,*
> *I would be happy to do it for you."*
> — GROUCHO MARX —

Towards the end of 2011, I was shifted down to central Queensland. I would be working in a live 66000V switchyard out at a place called Gracemere. This High Voltage substation is where the High Voltage incoming feeders would supply power to Rockhampton and surrounding areas. They had built the new infrastructure for the lines and towers to the western side of the substation, and we were installing all the PLC and control systems for the coal trains. The coal train lines came in from many directions to one feeder line to the coal ports near Rockhampton or Hay Point near Mackay.

Before working in coal, you have to have a coal board medical. This is a very different but stringent medical that lasts for five years. You also have to complete a Standard 11, a course that introduces you to the coal fields and the layout of the coal fields. Your fitness is checked vigorously by a physio and a chest x-ray is done and sent to the USA to be evaluated. This is to ensure you don't have black lung or any spots on your lung. In hard rock and surface mining, x-rays are also taken now.

The physicals can also be quite demanding as well, e.g., carrying weights, doing step ups, push ups, bench presses, squats, and climbing and on top of that taking an ECG.

Medicals for all mine sites are similar, but each mine requires their own medical. Honestly, I don't know how these big fat fellas pass some of these medicals and physicals, but they keep turning up. On top of all this are the mining company inductions. These can sometimes take up to two days to complete. Without these inductions validated, you cannot get access to the site.

For electricians, we have to keep our licences up to date. Licences in Queensland, Western Australia and Northern Territory last for five years then an online renewal is required. Also, to keep our licences current, we have to complete a CPR/LVR (Cardiac Pulmonary Rescue/Low Voltage Rescue) First Aid course. Other requirements are Confined Space certificates, Working at Height certificates, High Risk licences, Hazardous Area certificates, Instrumentation, High Voltage Switching Tickets, and Authorisation on Heavy Equipment. This list goes on. Every area of the plant has their own safety inductions as well.

Coal is very flammable and to see fires light up of coal stockpiles is not unusual on some occasions. Where there is coal, there is usually methane gas underground as well. I will talk about that later as I have worked as operator electrician on a methane gas plant.

Building the electrics in the switchyards for the coal trains went on well after I was asked to go to the coal maintenance team at one of the coal mines in central Queensland with the same company UGL.

We did have a few crazy fellas or one particular crazy fella in this switchyard I was working in. I cannot remember his name but he was really loopy. Where we had accommodation and living away allowance he would camp outside under the stars. Where we ate normal meals, he followed some guru that told him he had to blend and eat rolled oats for every meal and if he couldn't, he would self-inflate himself with liquid rolled oats. He was loud and, like most redheads, pretty aggressive. He did his work in wiring control systems in PLC boards and thought he was the best. Maybe he was.

One day, an old mate tried to catch me off guard. Around the perimeter of the fence line, there had been a number of snakes encroaching trying to get inside the fence and he was killing them off. These were brown snakes and very aggressive. So, one day he had this inclination to see what I would do if he walked up behind me with one of his dead trophy snakes and throw it in my direction. Remember even a dead snake still has venom. Well, he did just that, thinking I would jump, but the snake he threw missed me and I didn't jump. This took the wind out of his sails.

In that main switchyard, there were times Ergon Energy had opened and closed the main feeder breakers and we had to stand by. When these contacts are opening, there is a massive arc crossing between the contacts as they open and when they are closed again, you hear a big "BANG!"

So, you cannot be complacent where dangers can be extreme

in these yards. As I said before, you cannot save anyone else's life except your own if something goes wrong in one of these high voltage switchyards.

The roster we were on in Gracemere was a 10/4 roster, ten days on and four days off, drive in and drive out. I teamed up with another fella and it was an 800 km drive either way to and from Townsville.

Remember, this wasn't the only train HV switchyard that was being installed and commissioned. There were a number scattered all around the perimeters of the coal mines and train tracks.

There were a good few months in commissioning this project and then I would be off to the coal fields.

First port of call, as I had had an interview with UGL management and BMA (BHP and Mitsubishi Alliance) management, was Goonyella Riverside.

Goonyella Riverside Mine was situated about 10 kms north of a mining town called Moranbah. In this area, there are a number of coal mines. Remember these coal mines produce coking coal to make steel, very little for thermal. These mining companies BHP, Anglo-American and Glencore are both surface and underground with their own camps and facilities.

Trains would be loading up twice a day, sometimes more, on a ring railing system so the trains of course go into the train load out at the mine and out back onto the track it came in on. Every mine in the area has a similar set up, with trains being loaded up and then training to the coal ports 24/7.

At Goonyella Riverside, we maintained the conveyors, substations and wash plant where the coal has been crushed, screened and washed down, train load outs, stackers the grading stations which move up and down tracks, to all the switch boards and processing instruments, flotation ponds. Some of the conveyors would come up from underground tunnels so we had to have our confined space requirements up to date.

Not only is coal flammable and produces methane gas but it is also corrosive. Dust suppression is a big thing with sprinkler systems over stockpiles and water trucks on haul and mining roads.

Switch gear is cleaned regularly on maintenance shutdowns to prevent fires and explosions which I have seen on a few occasions. Coal dust seems to get into everything even through your clothes compared to hard rock dust. But nonetheless, dust is dust and I have been around when electrical switch gear has exploded due to dust build ups shorting out between live busbars taking out the main power.

Again, I had to do a pit pass out on a coal haul truck, two hour driving down in the open cut pit. I nearly fell asleep in this Cat Haul Truck. As my contract with UGL was fixed plant, I would never get to go down the pit again or at least the coal pit.

There was a fella by the name of Boofie, Big Scotty, another little fella can't remember his name, the supervisor and the UGL superintendent on our crew. This was Riverside. On the Goonyella side, there were about ten fellas and ten vehicles, and we only had one. We got really fit walking to maintenance jobs around the site.

Going down the coal tunnels where conveyors brought the processed coal from stockpiles above, where the coal was sifted through grids onto the conveyors and out to the train load, we had to radio control before we entered and exited the tunnels. We had to radio control also for safety as we entered and exited the decline under the floatation ponds for maintenance on the electric motors and the control systems.

These areas are classified as confined spaces with only one entry, sometimes two, on the other side of the coal tunnels if the vent door is open. With a confined space, you have to have a sentry at the entrance with a radio for safety observations. If he feels safety is compromised, he radios those down in the tunnel and gets everyone out. There is a register that all work groups sign as they enter and leave the tunnel and of course JHAs (Job Safety Analysis) is read, understood and signed by work crews also before entering any work front and signed off by supervisor. All these documents are legal documents and are retained and filed. If there is a safety breach or if there is a fatality, these documents are brought out in courts of law. Remember, where there is coal, there are gases. Confined spaces can be on any job front with only one entry and potential gases. So, it is important that persons are adequately trained before working in these areas and if they are not, they cannot enter the confined space.

If boilies are welding and there is no ventilation, the fumes can be overwhelming and deplete the oxygen levels. Any gases by natural underground deposits of hydrogen sulphide, which smells like rotten eggs, can deplete the oxygen levels and can also be quite dangerous. So, when dealing with coal, we are dealing with methane and fire ignition. With underground coal, high levels of oxygen with a slight ignition can also be very explosive.

Gas monitors are a requirement working in most confined spaces and underground now. They are carried by one person working in that area. Most monitors are able to pick up a range of gases and if levels get high for some reason, a flashing light with an audible alarm is set off. Thus, all persons must remove themselves from that area until the gas levels are reduced, or adequate ventilation is installed.

The safety for the mining resources follows a strict code of practice. If you don't follow them with all the paperwork, you are a danger to yourself and others and you should not be onsite.

I have seen tyre fires on haul trucks coming up from the pit. If this happens, it becomes an all-site emergency as any fire in coal can spread very quickly.

Getting back to our team of electricians, it was a close-knit team and we all worked together as a team. Booie was the funniest, he would have some preventative maintenance checks to do. In doing them, he would pull a conveyor pull chord switch to pieces or an MCC board partially to pieces and call up on the radio that he needed a hand to put things together as the time frame was running out and equipment needed to be livened up for production. He got into trouble a few times for doing this, but we helped him get it done. If there was anyone with too much attention to detail, it was Boofie. But in saying that, he did bring up some valid safety issues and actually some very good preventative maintenance issues, which were documented.

Big Scotty and I were working in the wash plant completing maintenance checks on the coal screens when one of the plant operators came up to us in a panic. The main MCC board or the main switch board on that level had big holes in the back of the cabinet, exposing live phase bars. The floor crew were hosing down as their concerns became apparent as they saw this major hazard. This is how corrosive coal can be.

I got a whole lot of bog and patched what I could see up and notified the supervisor of the hazard. This was done on the night

THE LUCINDA PORT INSURANCE ASSESSMENT

I was due to go home for my days off. When I got back four days later, the supervisor had not followed up the hazard; he was given a real dressing down and he tried to blame me for his incompetence. This was the beginning of a major feud between this fella and me.

From that day on, it was really unpleasant working with or around this fella. He made things quite difficult for a few of us.

Goonyella Riverside had two security gates. One for Riverside, which is the side we worked on, and one for Goonyella, which the other electrical and trades personnel for UGL worked on. The mining company BMA would only let us work a maximum of seventy-two hours a week straight. Any further hours had to be authorised. This was due to fatigue management. Most other sites, if our roster was 7/7, we did eighty-four hours as we were flown out. Coal roster is 4/4, drive in drive out. Most fellas lived in Mackay or surrounding areas. I of course lived in Townsville, and it was only a five-hour drive home.

Every Tuesday the fellas from Goonyella would come over to Riverside to help us with a maintenance shut and every Thursday we would be over at Goonyella helping with a maintenance shut on part of the plant. Remember, when we do a maintenance shut, that part of the plant isolated mechanical and electrically with full lockouts so equipment cannot not be started electrically or mechanically whist being worked on. Equipment can be cleaned, replaced or new installations are incorporated in maintaining production.

This day I was doing field tests with an electrical engineer, an old mate supervisor was patrolling the area looking for me. We had no vehicle. The engineer and I were walking through the coal mud to the MCC rooms switch board rooms. We got the work done, testing all the variable speed drives and programming as quickly as possible. Got out of there quickly. Went back and did all the paperwork. The supervisor was trying to call me up on the radio and I conveniently turned the radio down to finish paperwork. Strike two.

The following week, having completed all the maintenance at Riverside that week, on the Thursday coming, an all-day shut had been programmed in for the wash plant on two levels.

Another supervisor by the name of Trevor and I had been given list of maintenance checks and electrical motor disconnections and reconnections. We would complete these inspections, motor disconnections and reconnections by early afternoon. We then decided to find a quiet place and fill out all our paperwork in the cab of the Toyota ute. That quiet place happened to be behind a brick blast wall.

Well, next thing you know, Mr Patrolling Supervisor is driving around looking for us as he hasn't seen us all day and here they are behind this blast wall, not even knowing what we are doing. He sees us there.

Trevor doesn't like this guy either and he would never be confronted by Mr Supervisor.

In the meantime, the mines manager had taken a group of engineers into the new high voltage switchyard and had walked past us in the ute. There were no concerns as he was doing his thing and we were doing ours.

Well, the next day, I get summoned into the office for a review, not just me but Boofie to follow me.

This is how a fabrication of a situation started. Mr Supervisor was sitting in his chair, calm and collected, and the superintendent starts the conversation.

"We had a complaint from the mines manager yesterday that two fellas were asleep in a Toyota ute with seats reclined behind a blast wall."

"Who fabricated that?" I asked.

"You don't need to know," the superintendent commented.

I said, "I'm going to see the mines manager about this."

"You don't need to," the superintendent said.

"Yes, I do," I said.

At this point, he brings up this review thing and says, "We are

THE LUCINDA PORT INSURANCE ASSESSMENT

going to have to terminate your contract with the company."

"Fine," I said. "But I will be going to see the mines manager on my way out."

When the rest of company trades staff found out what had happened, they downed their tools, refused to answer the radio calls from Mr Supervisor, and called a meeting with management. It was an unfair and untruthful dismissal. Management wouldn't back down. To management, it was strike three.

At least I got the last laugh. The supervisors from BMA liked me being around and they also were not happy with my management. It wouldn't be that long that these two fellas got what came round later.

However, I did go and see the mines manager. I had no trouble with that at all. The day I was leaving, I made an on-the-spot appointment to see him and he was very welcoming. I introduced myself, told him a bit about myself, and then proceeded to tell him the situation.

I got straight to the point. I asked him, "Did you make a complaint yesterday about two fellas in a white Toyota ute behind a blast wall with the seats reclined, asleep?"

I told him we had seen him with a group of engineers walk into the new HV switchyard past us while we were writing out our paperwork.

He proceeded to tell me that was correct with the engineers. He then said, "If I had seen a white utility with fellas asleep in it, I would be banging on their window and asking in no uncertain terms what they were doing there."

Then I proceeded to tell him, "You have been implicated in a big lie that involves me and another company supervisor with a fabricated story to remove me from site by my management."

The mines manager said, "Son, I will definitely look into this and it will be a shame to see a good employee go."

I really got to understand that phrase, "He who laughs last has the last laugh." I had the last laugh with UGL at the time.

I finally asked him, "This will not have any bad come backs on my reputation in the coal mine sites?"

He said, "No. You did the right thing in standing up for what's ethical and right."

It is easy to go along with the crowd, but when you stand out to say something that's right, you are either standing alone or others are standing with you.

In this case, my work colleagues stood with me and when I came back a few years later to this site under different management, some of the fellas that stood with me were still there and were glad to see me. In that time working at Goonyella Riverside Coal, which would be one of the many coal mines I would work at, I had hired rental cars through my other business to travel to work. The rental company would keep extending my lease as I would never tell them where I was driving to. Maybe if they had known, they might have put the premiums up. By the time I left the mine, I had clocked up 14000 km on three different rental cars each, having driven all the back mining roads off the main road to and from Townsville.

The only conditions that were prevalent would be the weather in the wet season, which could be flash flooding, wildlife on the road and lightning strikes in the wet season also.

Kangaroos and livestock were the worst to hit on the road and I did hit kangaroos.

I would work with this international company again a few years later with new management and new opportunities. This little unfortunate circumstance did not faze me as I grew accustomed to the mining culture, especially when it came to management issues. Usually, better opportunities come and those that stay miserable do nothing about changing circumstances.

I think Boofie was given the same treatment but stayed for a little longer. He carried on with the crap I wouldn't take. Eventually he left. I met up with Boofie a few years later, still the same pedantic Boofie.

Success is stumbling from failure to failure with no loss of enthusiasm.
— WINSTON CHURCHILL —

The Mount Isa Switchyard Rebuild

I would be back on the road to Mount Isa for a hospital rebuild and building a new switchyard for Xstrata Mount Isa Mines as a contractor.

Being away from home certainly takes a toll on family life. I had two young women and my wife to contend with when I got home and certain times of the month with three women were not the easiest. It was lonely working those twelve-hour shifts, only to come back to your accommodation, have a meal, go to bed, start again at 6:00 a.m., then having to be up at 5:00 a.m., working till 6:00 p.m. sometimes up to three weeks if you are on mine construction with maybe two days off in between.

The maintenance shifts like the coal and century mine were the family-oriented shifts as you could be home every week, but they are still twelve-hour shifts days and nights.

This is a miner's life and it's taken a toll on a lot of work colleagues I have worked with. Men and women sacrifice the time away from home to make sure their families have everything provided for them. I can tell you, it is lonely for both spouses. The separation, the divorces, the suicides, the child support payments—even my marriage has suffered. All I could see was managing all the finances, my daughters' education, an apartment for the safety of my family whilst being away. Maybe like many of us, I did all the right things for the right reasons, but we let our relationships fail and, in the end, needed someone else's shoulder to cry on. I had to repair my marriage to save it and also repair the heartaches my daughters endured. These things take time, but we forgave each other. It was only through the grace of God this situation was healed.

We still have our problems, my wife and I, and will still journey

THE MOUNT ISA SWITCHYARD REBUILD

through life having to deal with stuff. But trust is a big thing in a relationship. Doubts can be there as well.

Mount Isa has become a familiar place to work again, and this time initially I would be on the electrical modification to the emergency and some of the surgical wards for the Mount Isa regional hospital. This time I would be on for about three months before working back on Mount Isa Mines as a subcontractor in building a high voltage substation for mines power. Also, we were making some overhead repairs on the 66000v lines in the number two switchyard for the mine's power.

In the new switchyard, we had to dig fuses together with special welds, earthing grids, criss-crossing right down the whole length and width of the switchyard—from fence to fence and bonding the fencing poles to the earth grid as well. This required about three five-hundred-meter drums of 120 mm 2 uninsulated copper cable. From the heavy generators that produce the power to the heavy transformers, the earthing bond is substantial. If you can imagine a transformer or an explosion from either, a massive current thousands of times greater than the output of the transformer or generator is produced and when or if this happens, that current goes directly to the earth grid and trips out any overhead or circuit breaker protection.

As you can imagine, the weight of this cable over a distance would be very heavy when rolling it off the drum, so a mobile machine helped to drag the cable where it needed to be positioned.

That was the first stage before all the concrete pads were installed for the power generators and transformers.

The next stage of the project, we had to bring transformers into the switchyard. These weren't small transformers either; they were 20-tonne transformers in 66000v switchyard, trucked in and craned off. Then the circuit breaker protection structure was brought in and assembled on the new concrete pads. In between those times, we were spending time in the number two concentrator switchyard, working on the overhead isolated feeder lines, replacing all the damaged insulators. On top of that, we had heavy lightning strikes. The severity of the damage on the vast area of the mine site had blown HV power poles to pieces. These poles were still smouldering days after the strike. Eventually all poles would become concrete poles to prevent decimation of wooden poles.

There were a few times a helicopter was called in to check the lines to see where the fault had taken place. Those times we were sent out to check would be in remote four-wheel drive areas up steep terrain.

The lines would many times be hanging off the poles. If you know anything about power lines spanning over distance, they are very heavy to lift. A block and tackle would be used to lift each individual line back up into position.

So in between building a switchyard, maintaining heavy switch gear in the number two concentrator yard and helping to fix damaged lines, we also had other projects on. One of these was running nearly 300 meters of a three-phase cable from the power source to a new way bridge for haul trucks and terminating both ends.

This was at another Xstrata mine 20 km down the road from Mount Isa Mines. We had to get a rock breaker to have a trench dug through the rock, so this was done for us. We also had turns in welding stands for cable trays all the way down the steep embankment, across the entry to the hole (the entry to the underground decline) and back down the other side of the embankment to the existing power.

Towards the end of that year, Xstrata were spending all their allocated budget monies to complete every project as at the beginning of the following year Xstrata would be bought by the new company Glencore as it still operates today.

Every day on entering the site at the George Fisher zinc mine, we had to change into clean overalls. This is what they call clean in clean out. At the end of the day, overalls got placed in the washing bag and you showered. The idea of this is that no lead or zinc dust is taken off site which could affect the community. At Mount Isa

THE MOUNT ISA SWITCHYARD REBUILD

Mines, working in the lead smelter or number two concentrator is even more stringent. A respirator must be worn, gloves, and hearing protection with overalls. When you came in for meals, you had to shower and put on clean overalls.

Getting back to George Fisher mine. In the change out, we had allocated lockers for our clean clothes. The locker that was allocated to me without knowing was infested with red back spiders. If you get bitten by one of these spiders, they can make you extremely sick. This day, I had gotten into the work vehicle to go home after changing. I had one or two of these nasties crawling up my shirt sleeve. Quickly, I stopped the vehicle, jumped out and brushed these things off.

The change out shed is apparently fumigated at certain times of the year to prevent the breeding of these nasties. I must have been around at the wrong time.

The second thing that happened in the change out was I had left my good watch in the top pocket of my overalls one night on change out. Realising this overnight, I went the next morning to the laundry staff to see if I could rescue it. They said, "Yes, we did find it," bringing a hundred different pieces out to me. They tried to hold their laughter back, saying, "I think this is what you were looking for"—my good Olympic watch, completely destroyed in the commercial washing machine.

I wasn't too impressed.

By the end of 2012, as mentioned previously, Xstrata was spending all its allocated budget money before the handing over of mining operations to Glencore the following year. In 2013, Glencore stopped all projects and concentrated on maintenance to compensate for losses in the takeover. For about two years, Glencore never spent any serious money till they had to and when things started needing serious attention.

In the new switchyard, a company called AGGREKO was hiring out fifteen 500 KVA generators to prove a temporary supply through the transformers to the HV lines, then to the mine's power. This was purposely done as the mine's power was load shedding to different parts of the plant as the Stanwell power station could not give the mines what was needed.

A new gas-fired power station was in the completion stage to provide the mines power exclusively for Mount Isa Mines and would be coming online within the next year, which was 2013. Mount Isa mines had already in recent years built a gas-fired generator plant behind X41, the underground part of site on the opposite side of the car parks. Amine requires a lot of power, a lot of water in the process and a lot of manpower, both surface and underground, to process the ore body.

I will talk about the two underground entries X 41 and R62 later when working underground.

Initially driving back to Townsville in a rental car from Mount Isa, having left the Isa in the early hours of the morning, I was on the other side of Cloncurry and a kangaroo jumped out and then jumped back in front of me. The left-hand side of the car was smashed, the kangaroo was killed. This would be my first experience of wildlife interaction on the main roads. It was another eight hours on the road to Townsville. Having arrived back around 10 a.m., I went straight to the Hertz rentals at the airport.

I went into the office and apologetically said, "Um, I have just hit a kangaroo and it's done a wee bit of damage."

The lovely lady I had been dealing with in the last year or so said, "You haven't got the full insurance coverage."

I was thinking this was going to hurt. Never think you are too careful you won't have an accident, even if you have been driving rentals great distances.

Michelle said, "Don't tell anyone but go to the panel shop where we take our cars to be fixed." And so I did. Instead of paying $3000 plus, it cost $1500 for repairs.

One thing I did learn from that experience is to get your own insurance coverage when hiring a rental car and in the words

THE MOUNT ISA SWITCHYARD REBUILD

of Monty Python's *Life of Brian*, "Always look on the bright side of life."

In 2012, on one of my breaks, I would be flying to New Zealand for my daughter Rachel's 21st birthday in Tauranga. Rachel had gone back to live in Tauranga, New Zealand for three years as initially she didn't settle very well in Aus and missed her friends. Within three years, Rachel would be back in Aus as she also missed family and would become a much stronger and outgoing young woman.

Anyways, I had decided to take the afternoon off to catch the 6:00 p.m. Qantas flight out of Mount Isa. Contractors had been working on the runway lights and had a problem trying to get them back on. The lights operate from an automatic switch. The pilot can switch them on from inside the cockpit by clicking five times on his radio transmitter button. I used this system myself in New Zealand at remote aerodromes and on occasions here in Australia.

We boarded the flight and I think we waited an hour on board, then had to disembark as the runway lights had still not been fixed. We waited in the terminal another four-and-a-half hours, having had a meal provided by Qantas and then by midnight the pilots had run out of duty hours, the lights still not working.

We had to make our way back to the camp, courtesy of Qantas. Had to reschedule connecting flights, having nearly lost them all.

The good thing about this, a Virgin flight booking consultant felt sorry for me and held the booking out of Brisbane, placing me in business class, which sounded good to me.

So, the Saturday morning, I left Mount Isa in a hurry to catch the Brisbane flight to Auckland. A quick trip in the shuttle bus and I made it to my sister's place in Tauranga for Rachel's 21st birthday. WHEW.

This is just another of the challenges I faced when flying out and into Australia. But wait, there is more. Rachel did get to have a great 21st with all her friends and family meeting up. Good on you, Rachel.

The Beginning of the Flying Tradesmen Partnership

It was during this time at Mount Isa I had been living at the Irish club when a room in a four-bedroom house became available. With cheaper rent, furniture and reasonable kitchen facilities, I thought it wasn't a bad deal, as the fella that was subleasing the house off Isa Skills had his own employee in the house, me and a mining field mechanic. Isa Skills had one of their personnel in there as well.

The fella that was an employee was a young man by the name of Roy Randal. I will use his real name as he became a friend and business partner.

Mr Dunstan had a so-called aviation company, which we will call Outback Aviation. This company flew to the indigenous settlements outside Mount Isa. Roy had been one of the pilots flying on

THE FLYING TRADESMEN PARTNERSHIP

charter operations for this company for some months. However, his contract had been abruptly terminated and he was told to leave the premises where we were living.

Mr Dunstan even came around to the house to make sure he was gone as he had negotiated a contract with another fella.

I stood by Roy and although he would be going back to South Australia for the Christmas period, he approached me before he left, asking whether I would take him on as an electrical apprentice. We could start a business. Roy had some very good business skills on paper, and I had the expertise on the technical side.

I was very hesitant at first as it was a big commitment. But we did it.

It was a rocky start at first as Glencore had taken over Mount Isa Mines. They spent nothing for the next two years on any upgrades so contractors had minimal work.

Two things happened, we set up a business called the Flying Tradesmen with the idea of servicing as many cattle stations in Northwest Queensland by air and road, and tendering for small mining contracts.

First thing we did after setting the business up with a name and Roy signing the electrical apprenticeship papers with Mygate (the electrical apprenticeship company that oversees the correct training both in theory and hosting) was to fly down to Adelaide to pick a work ute that had been leased to us. We drove this Nissan Navara all the way back to Mount Isa via port Augusta, Coober Pedy (a town famous for its opals) through to Alice Springs, Northern Territory to Tennant Creek, Northern Territory to Mount Isa, Queensland. It was roughly 3000 km in three days and we carried extra diesel with us for the very long stretches of road in between populated areas. This is Australia. No matter where you travel, east to west, the distances are very great on the road.

So, we got to the Isa with a ute. We established about 1000 cattle stations on our data bank and started working remote. Just before we drove the ute up from South Australia, we hired a Toyota four-wheel drive land cruiser to drive all the way east to Julia Creek. Julia Creek is roughly 260 kms. By the time we reached Julia Creek Township, it was quite dark, and we still had to travel inland a bit to find Lands End Station. There were kangaroos all over the road, and at 60 kms, we hit not just a kangaroo but a rather large kangaroo. Roy had been driving and I think he was a little shaken. I would continue to drive.

We actually demolished the kangaroo and completely bent the bull bar at the front. No panel damage was done but when we did take the land cruiser back to the rental company, it cost us the excess of $1300 to pull out and straighten the bull bar.

However, we did get to Lands End Station that night. The owners were waiting for us with a very nice meal.

The following day, we were refitting switch gear inside the main homestead, station accommodation, farm sheds including broken overhead power cables, outside lighting. We spent a good two days working around the cattle station. Completing everything on the owners list, we packed up and drove back to the Isa. On the way back, driving back to the main highway, the carcass of the dead kangaroo we hit had been picked clean by eagles and scavengers. That's within two days.

Roy and I did have some fun. Roy was a quiet and pedantic young man. I am very outgoing and confident. We worked as a team

THE FLYING TRADESMEN PARTNERSHIP

in those years. We did get round the cattle stations in Northwest Queensland by road and air, as the name suggests, THE FLYING TRADESMEN. Initially, we had a single engine piper Cherokee we loaded our tools into. Then Roy was able to lease a twin-engine high wing Partonavia aeroplane from South Australia. He flew with the owner initially up to Mount Isa as the plane would be based at Mount Isa on a full lease.

Both Roy and I are commercial pilots, at the time Roy being more current as we say in aviation terms and I had just completed my currency checks.

So, we removed four of the seats and left one spare, making a big cargo hold for all our gear. We had planned to fly into cattle stations that were pretty remote as their airstrips were 800 meters or longer and were maintained for the RFDS (Royal Flying Doctor Service). Let me tell you, if there is any charitable organisation to support, it is the RFDS. They are an amazing service that saves lives in the outback.

The house we were renting off Mr Dunstan in Mount Isa, he was subleasing off Isa Skills. This became a problem. Mr Dunstan hadn't paid the rent for a while and had an outstanding amount of $5000. Receiving a phone call from Isa Skills this day, we were told we all had to be out of the house within the day. I had to renegotiate the lease as there was me and three others in the house, not including the Isa Skills employee. The mining mechanic Justin was on shift. In the end, Isa Skills accepted our terms. They had put the rent up to recuperate their losses as we later found out by the owner who lived in America. The rent he was given and the rent we were paying to Isa Skills had a margin on it.

The tables were turned now, and Mr Dunstan still had an employee in the house under our lease and he had to try and negotiate with us to keep his employee in the house. The Isa Skills employee had moved out and Roy moved back in. Eventually Mr Dunstan's employee had had enough and left as well. The only thing left was the Outback Aviation company car. Roy and I decided to hang onto it to recuperate some of the rent losses. Mr Dunstan was not too happy with this idea and harassed us to get his car back. So, we went down to the police station and asked where we stood with the law on outstanding rent and holding on to his car. Police advised, technically he is the owner, and he could file a charge that we were holding onto it illegally.

So, if we couldn't get our rent money, we would turn the tables again. Mr Dunstan was flying a man up from Brisbane to drive back the white Hyundai car. We had both sets of keys. We then parked the car in a car park in town, waited for the fella to fly up to Mount Isa and then posted the keys standard post to Brisbane. This fella would have to fly back to Brisbane then fly back to Mount Isa and drive the sixteen hours back to Brisbane. Honestly, I don't think the car was worth the hassle, but Roy and I had the last laugh.

Also, Mr Dunstan was a gun collector and had previously had guns and ammunition locked away in a gun cabinet. He had removed this from the premises before he himself had left living at the premises. What he didn't remove was a single barrel shot gun in pieces in a bag in one of the wardrobes.

Roy and I were cleaning out his unwanted gear when we came across this weapon in a bag. So, I immediately went down to the police station and handed over this gun.

Immediately I was questioned as though I was the bad guy. "Where did you get this, who does it belong to, whereabouts did you find it?"

All I said was, "I'm handing in a gun, it was left in the wardrobe where I live. The previous occupier was a gun collector, and—" (I had to rub it in)—"he was an ex-copper as well and that's all I know. This is his name. Mr Dunstan. Runs an aviation company out of Isa." For some reason, after giving these details for the next six months, I kept getting these phone calls from the Mount Isa police about the acquisition of this gun. I didn't know if I hadn't explained it clearly, they didn't understand my writing or if the gun belonged to Ned Kelly.

THE FLYING TRADESMEN PARTNERSHIP

Eventually they must have figured it out.

I did have another friend from New Zealand who carried a magnum .44. He was licensed to only fire this at a gun club firing range. Ian gave me this handgun to pick up one day. I couldn't believe how heavy this slab of metal was. You really had to hold it with two hands. I know if I had fired this gun, the recoil would have thrown me backwards in a big way.

My only gun training was in air cadets where I learnt to fire .303 rifles very accurately. Apart from that, I have never had an inclination to demolish anything with a high-power gun.

Roy and I completed a number of contracts on cattle stations, mine sites and in Mount Isa itself. He did gain good electrical experience over those years and learnt to be independent as well as learning from various other trades people when I wasn't around. Roy picked up people skills, which is lacking in young people today and is so important to learn. Also he built confidence in himself at the same time.

What I learnt from Roy as he still works on me today is computer skills, always finding the best deals, never outlay more than you have to. It has been a little frustrating for me sometimes as paperwork is not always my priority. Roy is very patient in that area with me.

From 2013 to 2017, we flew thousands of kilometers around North Queensland. It was always work-related. During those years, station owners were facing severe drought and it was heartbreaking. We did the very best we could in providing a very affordable service, traveling huge distances in outback Queensland. My young friend did a lot of planning and I negotiated with clients.

We even picked up some mining contracts, having completed and submitted some substantial paperwork for access to sites, insurance we had to have and payment schedules for those mines. Camp maintenance was one of our most lucrative contracts. We tended for and did the testing of electrical equipment and injection testing of all breakers in every camp switchboard. Onsite, I was authorised to work on the processing side of most North Queensland mines. This would be from the field to the processing of the ore body.

There were months I would be away working on construction of building mine sites, especially coal.

I had to live on borrowed money on four credit cards at this time, as work wasn't always consistent. We were renting a bigger apartment in Townsville for the family, renting my own apartment out to the military, renting this house at Mount Isa and trying to keep payments going for my house in New Zealand. Initially I had long term tenants in New Zealand until the couple decided to split. The house remained empty and I was paying this high mortgage. This bank had done an unscrupulous thing by making my payments on completely fixed interest. When the interest on repayments became low, I was paying the fixed interest at a higher rate on both loans. I won't tell you what bank it was but can give you a hint. It starts with A and finishes with Z.

Eventually, no matter how hard I worked away from home, I lost my house in New Zealand. But with some careful planning and a good budget my young friend put together, I paid all these debts off. It took two big mining construction jobs. I built the electrical construction on a new coal mine, Caval Ridge, for the mining company BMA, and also the expansion to the coal terminal port Hay Point for coal shipping. At the same time, my young friend was trying to keep himself employed with one my colleagues at Mount Isa and we were trying to maintain The Flying Tradesmen contracts as well.

Building the electrical construction for Caval Ridge Coal Mine was a three-week on, seven-day off roster for five months.

We on the electrical and mechanical team were working and commissioning one of the main crushers, three main conveyors as well as building the electrics to 3 MCC switchboard rooms and commissioning.

These were ten-hour days after every thirteen days, one day

THE FLYING TRADESMEN PARTNERSHIP

stand down. After the following thirteen days, we would be on our way home for a break. Qantas Airways were contracted to fly us directly back to Townsville. It would also be on this site I would become acquainted with a young fella called James Bolger. Under unusual circumstances, I would be his alarm clock, getting him up and making sure he had breakfast and never missed the bus that left at 5:00 a.m.

James would also become a valued friend. James is one of the *Band of Brothers*. We catch up every so often to discuss future work and have a social get together either in Townsville or Cairns.

It was during this period of time, I was able to access a privately owned aircraft C182 at the Moranbah airport. Moranbah is a privately owned airport owned by BMA (BHP and Mitsubishi Alliance) so every time a private flight is to take off and land, you have to get written permission from the head office in Brisbane. This I did by filling out forms, scanning and emailing. I was allocated slots on certain evenings as there were scheduled Qantas and Virgin flights coming in every day.

The aircraft itself had been left with very little fuel in it, so I had to borrow two helicopter Gerry cans from a local helicopter operator, use the company car and drive to Clermont 100 km away where I could fill up at the airport there with 100 litres of aviation fuel and drive back to Moranbah to fuel up aircraft. Having fuelled aircraft and waiting for the eligible slots after work, I did a number of flights over the coal mine areas, taking three of my work colleagues on each flight.

Everything was going alright till one night I lost radio contact with ARO (the Airport Runway Officer) so was radioing Brisbane Area to give my position and advise I had lost contact with Moranbah ground. In flying this day, I was positioning myself away from scheduled traffic then proceeded to land.

Having landed, the ARO expressed his concern as I had advised what had happened with radio. He was not impressed and complained to BMA, not even considering the standard safety precautions I had made while keeping required distances and height from scheduled aircraft.

Going back to having to work this project, we did get through this period. It was tough on my family. But still, we had our own apartment in Townsville and decided to cut our losses, break the lease upstairs and shift in downstairs once again.

The reason I am writing this is that sometimes life is tough, or unfair; people don't always understand your situation unless they have experienced it for themselves. God gives us the wisdom and the right people in our path if we trust him. I might not have always done the right things, but he has always been there for me.

At the beginning of 2014, I was contracted to G and S engineering under Bechtel Construction, completing a coal terminal upgrade for BHP at Hay Point south of Mackay. The wharf had been extended and three new shipping berths had just been or were in the process of being completed and we were commissioning the new onshore conveyors and main switchboard rooms for the plant. We not only had to carry security access to be onsite but we also had to have an MSIC card (Maritime Security Card). This is required for any persons working on wharves around Australia. An ASIC (Airport Security Card) is required for working on all airports in Australia. Without them, you don't have access unless escorted.

There were ten of us on our crew and we would be securing and testing all circuits and connections right back to the switch rooms with 240v supply and 24v supply for the PLC circuits.

We had a problem though. Most if not all the electrical equipment had been manufactured and assembled in China and was not up to Australian and New Zealand electrical standards. In other words, it was dangerous to the degree of water penetration through electrical fittings and chafing on cables without the plant even running. There were other issues as well. This was taken up with management as signing off was on our electrical licences and we were responsible if anything happened electrically. We as electricians have an electrical regulations book, codes of practice and Australian standards we adhere to. This was pointed out to management.

With union representation, we advised that all ten of us could not proceed unless we had a letter from the engineer responsible that he would be responsible for all the commissioning work to be completed with the standard of equipment being acceptable. This he did and I still have that letter today.

The project we did finish. There was only one near fatality on the wharf where someone nearly got crushed by a slab of concrete walling, but fortunately there was an obstruction that broke the fall and the person only received broken limbs. Of course, an investigation was made but the final report did not come out till months later.

Our supervision was really great, and safety procedures were followed very well. When we did finish our part of the project, we left knowing we had done every part of our work professionally and with the paperwork signed off. There would be no come backs on any of us.

Most days on this project we were up at 4 a.m. with breakfast and getting ready to leave by bus at 5 a.m. We were leaving site at 6:00 p.m. If you can imagine six to seven 50 to 60-seater Greyhound buses taking us from camp to site each day and back, stopping at security to tag our MSIC and port security tag. This was every day and the thirteenth day was a stand down day. Then we would be flown home for a seven-day break.

As I said, no one passes through the port facilities gate without MSIC and we wear these on us all the time.

One of the best things I looked forward to was playing my cornet in church cathedrals. I was able to get on the bus going into Mackay Town from the camp to attend this church and when I played in this cathedral, the sound of a brass instrument was magnificent. It was like playing a trumpet concerto in the brilliance of great acoustics.

The people in the church always welcomed me to the fellowship.

On a few occasions, I was invited out to lunch with the locals, which made the day enjoyable. As you can see, I was able to have some sort of life whist away from family working.

We did finish all our work by mid-2014 and when we had finished commissioning, we had notification from management to stay on to finish substation upgrades. There were the few of us that would. I was committed to moving on with another company project.

By mid-2014, I had been asked to join a team of electricians to complete a five-week maintenance shutdown at Phosphate Hill Mine 166 km south of Mount Isa.

We were flown in from Townsville directly on a mining charter. On previous occasions, I had done shift covers at the camp and on the mine site, so it was a familiar site to work on. The whole production plant was shut down for five weeks to do some serious maintenance on the acid plant, HV switching stations and the processing upgrades. We installed generators all over the plant to connect temporary power for all the essential services, including power for all the trades, offices and control rooms to keep the turbines running.

I must admit, this was a good site to work on and very well-organised. From pre-start meetings at 6:00 a.m. where all our safety briefs and hand overs from night activities were acknowledged and followed on for work activities during the day, most of our work was changing out pressure and flow meters, generator connections, temporary power supplies to buildings, electric motor testing and recording any faults.

We had some funny fellas working with us. One fella used to call me Spinner because I used to wind him up. He superglued my gloves to the side of my helmet and then superglued all these orange shrouds to the top of my helmet so it looked like a big spike. It looked like something out of the movie *Dumb and Dumber*, something Jim Carrey would wear. Anyways what goes round comes round. The electrical workshop was way out the back. It

THE FLYING TRADESMEN PARTNERSHIP

had an outside toilet attached to it and every morning at the same time, this fella would make his pilgrimage. It just so happened this morning after the event from the following day there were some rather large stones around the perimeter of this toilet. Waiting for the door to be locked and a minute or so to drop his tweeds, I threw a couple solid stones to hear his reply, "F......K." He had jumped off the toilet. When he came out a little flustered, we asked him if everything was alright, trying to hold back a laugh.

We always have some fun away from management and mostly out of sight so we don't get into trouble.

After five weeks, the plant was up and running. We had decommissioned the generators and temporary buildings. Production of phosphate in the main plant was in full swing. We were flown out on the mining charter back to Townsville.

Towards the end of 2014, nearly Christmas, Roy and I were in Townsville. We had driven the ute in from the Isa and were working on some projects when we got a call from the council shire at Lake Nash. This is a small aboriginal settlement at the bottom of the Northern Territory. We had flown out there from the Isa a number of times as the builder was a friend of Roy's and he had given some electrical work to us.

The night before, the main switchboard at the council offices had exploded. There was no power anywhere to the essential services. The back-up emergency generator could not come on because there was a complete meltdown at the board. The night we got the call both Roy and I were in Townsville. Quickly, I rang all my electrical friends to see if they would like to go for a bit of an adventure and fly out with Roy from the Isa on my behalf as two days later I would be flying to Perth and the up to the Pilbaras for maintenance shutdown at BHP YANDI mine. My offer was declined so Roy and I drove the ute all that night back to Mount Isa (1000 kms east), had a sleep for a few hours when we got there. Then loaded up the aircraft early afternoon, flight planned and flew to Lake Nash.

When we got there later in the day, we were taken straight to the offices of the council shire and what we saw, we couldn't believe. The council offices had not burnt down. Some electrical company had installed all these air conditioning units on the one phase. There were three phases over the whole building to balance the load and they overloaded a complete phase with an enormous amount of current. This high current drawn by the air conditioning systems would be more than what the cable was rated at and of course with overbearing current, it would eventually cause a fire.

It was getting dark so we couldn't do much. The power had been isolated from the pole as the main fuses had been pulled by the supply authority. We would strip the board in the morning and commence major repairs. What we did do that night was repair some equipment at the power station before getting a good night's sleep.

GO........OOOOD MORNING, LAAAKE NASH

Roy and I went down to the office, opened the board up and completely stripped it. We cut out everything burnt and re-joined all the circuits, replacing any burnt-out cables. We spent half the day repairing, replacing RCD breakers, the damaged main switch on board and advised them that the switchboard would have to be upgraded. We also redistributed the electrical load between the three phases on the board, and tested every circuit to make sure there were no faults. Also we made repairs on the emergency generator.

Having completed this by early afternoon, we repaired a chiller at the local store, went back and printed out all the paperwork at the builder's place for the supply authority in Darwin.

The fuses were reinstated on the pole. The council had their power back on. Everyone went back to work. We packed up our gear and flew out by 4 p.m., and were back at Mount Isa by 5:30 p.m. I was hoping to catch a flight back to Townsville that night. Apparently it was a bit late to check in so I would fly out the following morning. I would be in Townsville for the following night, saying hello to my wife and then flying to Perth and then up to area C BHP mine in the Pilbaras next day to commence seven nights on maintenance shift.

The Pilbaras are north of Perth, a two-hour flight to roughly any of the mining airports scattered up there. This is a big iron ore mining area with BHP, FMG, RIO TINTO, ROY HILL, and a number of copper and lithium mines up there as well. It is an all-day flight from Townsville with stops in Brisbane and Perth. This was also a very long week as we had already driven 1000 kms to the Isa, flown ourselves another 800 km there and back to Lake Nash, working all day making repairs, flying back to Townsville, and then flying to Area C Mine in the Pilbaras.

Finishing seven nights at Area C for BHP, I flew back to Perth, Brisbane and then to Mount Isa. I slept all the way on all flights as I was exhausted. The first part of the week was not planned for as it was an emergency call out. The Flying Tradesmen had kept its assurance that we would make the effort if there was an emergency.

When arriving back in Mount Isa, I slept for another four hours and then went to work with Roy to finish rewiring an engineering workshop that had fallen into disrepair. By this time, it was two days before Christmas 2014. I could not get a reasonably priced flight back to Townsville and our aircraft had run out of hours so I had to catch the Greyhound bus back to Townsville, another twelve hours.

In 2015 it seemed even busier. The Flying Tradesmen had picked up mining contracts at Phosphate Hill Mine and I was helping with shift covers at the camp. This would be filling in for staff either sick or taking holidays. The camp maintenance was a good place to work. You worked on your own. You would have call outs, kitchen break downs with appliances, installation work, and preventative maintenance checks. If you had all your work done, you would go and help loading and unloading of aircraft coming and going. You had your own vehicle and a workshop to work out from. Sometimes I gave the other maintenance fellas a hand if needed.

The good thing about this swing mit was a 7/7 roster, home every week, whereas on construction you could be away up to three or four weeks at a time. Also, camp staffing is a lot smaller, so everyone generally knows everyone on either shift.

The company is IPL (Incitec Pivot Limited), an international company. It had spent a lot of money in recent years upgrading the camp facilities and the plant itself. So, a lot of the gear was new. IPL also ran the sulphuric acid plant at Mount Isa Mines, which produces sulphuric acid to produce fertiliser and also trains sulphuric acid to Sun Metals acid plant Townsville for the zinc galvanisation process.

I had been working some shift covers early 2015 when one night, I collapsed. I completely lost my balance and was sweating profusely and vomiting. The nurse saw my condition and helped me to the bathroom to cool me down. At this point, I couldn't get up and was vomiting even more and started to shiver. The nurse then called the paramedics and then the RFDS (Royal Flying Doctor Service). The nurse and the paramedics kept talking to me, making sure I hadn't lost consciousness, and kept me warm. Then when the RFDS flew in at 11:30 p.m. that Saturday night, I was transferred from the paramedic vehicle to the plane and wrapped in tin foil to keep me warm. Not to go in an oven. I was then flown to Mount Isa Airport where an ambulance was waiting to take me to the hospital. By the way, the RFDS is one of the best services Australia has for flying critical and sick people to major centres with nurses and doctors.

The nurse at the camp thought I had a stomach ulcer. I was very dehydrated as well and they inserted a drip into each of my arms. Management could not get ahold of my wife or my family so Roy was the only known contact. At 2:00 a.m., he came and stayed with me till I was released the next day. I had to fly back to Phosphate to catch the mining charter back to Townsville the next day, which was the Monday. The camp staff had brought all my gear out to the airport and was loaded up with all the other bags.

THE FLYING TRADESMEN PARTNERSHIP

I couldn't come back to site until my stomach had been checked. That meant having a tube with a camera dropped inside me. The results said that I had a slight tear in my stomach, nothing serious though. With that confirmation, I was able to go back to Phosphate Hill for the next swing. At the same time, I was still able to carry on with maintenance shutdowns for BHP in Western Australia under Downer EDI mining.

It was on this maintenance shutdown at BHP Area C Mine, we had been indirectly working with a team of HV electricians from one of the HV switching companies. They had finished their work and were heading back to Perth. A day or two later, one of these fellas would be dead and three seriously burnt in hospital. One young fella later died in hospital from serious burns to 80% of his body. These fellas had been working in a shopping centre substation. They had been working near an electrical transformer when it exploded. I don't know the full details, but I can tell you, working with switch gear as often as I and many others do or have done, we should never be complacent, even with all the paperwork and safety procedures in place. If something is not right or anyone breaches any procedure, he or she should be removed from area. Work should be stopped and questions asked as they are endangering everyone else on the work front.

All the electrical crews I have worked with, everyone has looked after each other. This is a code of commitment and respect we have for each other. We also make sure we look after each other as in the mining environment, it is lonely at times. Working in remote areas for days or sometimes weeks at a time away from families can take a toll not only physically but emotionally as well.

The heat, the flies, the travelling continuously, the shifts between night and days just to provide for families is incredibly harsh. But on the other side, many qualifications are obtained, friendships are built, and you can have a lot of fun, especially if you're working with me and fun after hours if we are not too tired.

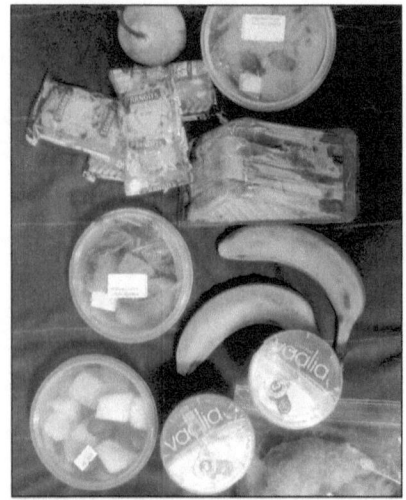
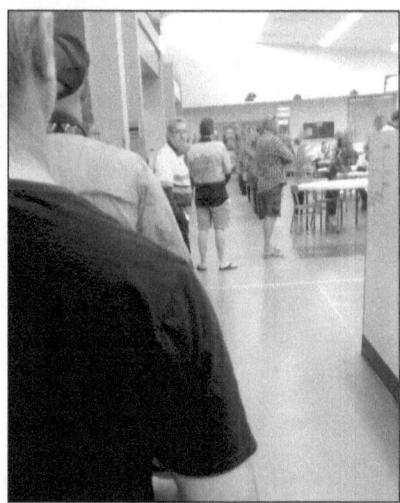

THE FLYING TRADESMEN PARTNERSHIP

Variety is the spice of life, I say. Don't remain in one place forever. I have never gone to any work front without committing the day in prayer.

> *The best advice I've received is*
> *"no one else knows what they're doing either."*
> —RICKY GERVAIS—

Coming back from the Pilbaras, Western Australia is an all-day event and I will talk about delayed flights later along this mining journey. I feel a bit like Forrest Gump, telling every detail of my journey. Anyway, it's fun. Criss-crossing Australia a number of times and living in and out of the Qantas club at the airports around Australia is not for everyone. But if your work is held up or a bit slow in one state, you travel interstate with all your licences and tickets.(But today, as I write this, April 2020, I'm stuck and cannot go home as they have closed the Western Australia and Queensland border due to the coronavirus.)

In March 2015, I was asked to go back to Mount Isa Mines and work on the hoisting maintenance with a company called Bear Instrumentation. This again would be one of my enjoyable contracts, although I would be living locally two weeks at a time in a house rented to The Flying Tradesmen in Mount Isa.

I renewed my underground inductions for hard rock as I had not been down the hole at Mount Isa Mines for some years. The last time I went down the hole, not being acclimatised, I landed up in hospital, dehydrated. In the last few years, I had been underground in other mines but Mount Isa was very deep and hot and I would have to watch my dehydration levels.

Another benefit of being down the hole is that it is fully air conditioned; switch gear gets very hot and without adequate ventilation, electrical equipment can trip out due to heat, components can burn out, and in the worst case scenario, overheating can cause electrical fires. The benefit for myself and others was that we could go in and cool down when necessary. The operator cabs downstairs were also air conditioned and we would use them to our advantage also.

A pre-start in the electrical hoisting workshop would commence at 6:00 a.m. and preventative maintenance checks and hand overs from night shift were acknowledged. If there had been a major breakdown, either mechanical or electrical, for some hours we were also advised and repairs would be followed up quickly. If down time on equipment had been more than ten hours, we would certainly have an inquiry come through from Switzerland about what was going on.

So, in this role, I would be moving to different levels, checking the electrics on the winders from the switch boards on the surface, the electric generators for the winders, racking in and out the HV switch gear to isolate equipment, especially the winder motors which carried the ore to the surface. Then we would harness ourselves on a platform fitted to the top of the cage that carried miners to different levels to check the cables going down the shaft. The fitters would check the mechanical structures as well. With the continual blasting that takes place on the lower levels twice daily between the hours of 8 a.m. and 8 p.m. at the lower levels, the shaft gets a hammering.

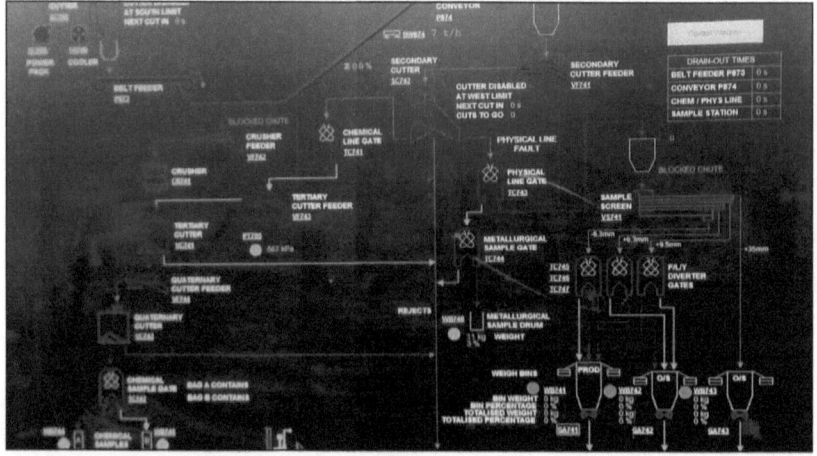

The cage goes down to level 21 and stops there. From level 20 down to level 33, which is where the ore crusher is, we would have a platform placed on the skip bin and ride that from level 20 to level 33. The light as you went down even further would become a small speck until eventually it disappeared. I never got down to the blasting level as you had to have a reason to go down there. We also did maintenance on the crusher and all the instrument levels and calibration checks. This is essential as weights measured for ore going to surface and the reading given on the telemetry systems had to be accurate.

The days we were down underground, we would take the cage or flee. (The flee was a smaller lift and took eight fellas on top and eight on the bottom.) We would rocket down the shaft to level 21 where we picked our work vehicle. The cage also goes down the shaft quite fast as well.

From level 21 with all our gear for the day, we drove the different levels to various workshops and operators' cabs. It was in the operators' cabs, we were able to cool off as mentioned before when we had finished our preventative maintenance checks.

With hard rock, there can also be rock falls. The ceiling down the declines and work areas are caged and bolted. The walls are coated with a mixture of cement and ore dust down the decline. Rock doctors are always checking for cracks and rock falls.

We did happen to have a boulder fall out of the wall near one of the winders during the time I was underground, something like a 10-tonne boulder just fell to the floor from the wall. Fortunately, no one was there when it happened, but it did cause some damage to the side of the operator's cab.

Safety again is taken very seriously and in the time Mount Isa Mines has been operating, a fatality is very rare. But in saying that, a fella that had been checking stopes, which are placed in walls after an area has been blasted, hadn't returned to the surface one day. His vehicle had been left empty and no one could find him. It would be weeks before his body was found. He had fallen down in

between two stopes. This is why electronic access is so important when entering and leaving underground so every person is accounted for and also blasting cannot take place till everyone is out or in a safe working area underground. If someone leaves without swiping out on their access, questions are asked as this holds up production. It can be a sackable offence.

Interesting to note: when they commence blasting underground between the hours of 8 a.m. and 8 p.m., everyone underground in safe working areas and the town rocks with the blast. You could be sitting in the Irish club having a meal and you get this jolt.

Some levels were not used anymore and workshops had been left with mechanical equipment still there, but the radio huts were still on some of these levels and still in service, so access was still required.

We also had access to the emergency escape ladders that lead to the surface. You could walk back up the levels from the 33 to level 21 through the access stairwell, which winds its way up. Remember that a few times you became very fit, kitted up with your underground belt, which carried your battery pack with a pager

THE FLYING TRADESMEN PARTNERSHIP

with cap lamp connected, your emergency kit on the other side of the belt.

We could also walk up some of the access roads, keeping out of the way of traffic. I would emphasise some, not all, because there is a lot of heavy earth moving machinery down there.

Two-way communication is very important underground, as being in contact with operators on mobile equipment, contact with surface operations and also a certain channel is dedicated for emergency and mines rescue. That channel is kept clear all the time.

The fellas and women I worked with were very skilled. Most of us were instrument technicians as well so maintaining the pressure, flow, weights, and the telemetry were also a big part of operations.

There were also days on the surface we had to look after the equipment in the winder operators tower and also the skip bin towers as I liked to call them, the odd occasion wiring in new switch boards in adjacent sheds to the electrical workshop.

On our crew, we had Tim the tool man as supervisor, a nice fella; Raymond, my South African buddy; Undies, a shift electrician; LeeRoy Whaler, a supervisor from way back who liked to make a point of testing everyone's electrical knowledge; Big Jeff who was with the same company as me who had been around Mount Isa Mines a long time and a fella who liked to have few laughs like myself; Trevor, Lesa, Jacinta, two women trades persons and two apprentices. Cannot forget Georgey, the other shift electrician, and an old fella called Tracy. A fairly full team.

We worked as two crews, which covered R62, the main cage and flee; P62, the skip that rocketed the ore from the bottom to the surface; X 41, which was the cage on the other side of the mine; the crusher on level 33; and all the levels in between, including the levels over at X41. So, you can see we covered a wide area of floor space.

We could drive a fair distance underground as there is around 10 km of roading down there. I think it takes over an hour now to get to the bottom of the underground. As I said, I have only been down to level 35 and there are about another five levels further. The blasting is done at the very bottom of the mine.

You can actually drive from where R62 cage stops to the bottom of X41 cage, as everyone had to do after a miners' incident one sunny day.

The winder operators drive the cages up and down the shafts as they do the skip bins. The cages and the flee go down around 6:00 a.m. and come back up 6:00 p.m., with miners on the top and bottom of the cage and two-way communication by radio inside the cage and the flee. Explosives and equipment are taken down at various times during the day and even light vehicles and machinery are taken down on the cage as required.

It is a different world down there and very busy.

The flee is probably used more during the day with personnel coming up and going down the shaft to level 21. At the same time, they had been installing the new electrical upgrade for the power and PLC systems to the running of the cage and the flee, replacing 1960s technology. This has taken a number of years in the process of completing this project.

Going back to the miners' incident one sunny day, the cage was brought to the surface for fitters to complete monthly maintenance inspections. Prior to commencing maintenance, four wedge blocks are placed in each outside corner of the cage before work takes place. Remember, no work can take place until JSA (Job Safety Analysis) has been completed and signed off by the supervisor. Fitters were harnessed above the cage, checking the hydraulics above and below the cage.

This day one of the wedges slipped out of position. The fitters fell back on their safety harnesses, one injuring himself, falling backwards and hitting himself as the wedge fell like a trajectory down the shaft, bouncing off all walls. Everyone on different levels heard this missile coming and ducked for cover. Remember, this is a long way down and the noise would have been very loud. The shaft was closed all day as an investigation had to take place. That night every miner had to be driven over to the other side of the mine and come up on the X41 cage as R62 incident was under investigation. The following day, we were riding the top of the cage going down the R62 shaft. The fitters were harnessed on, checking the structural integrity of the shaft, and I was checking the electrical cables going down the shaft for any damage from the wedge block. Fortunately, there was nothing serious.

As I have stressed, safety is taken seriously and unfortunately, human error cannot always be eliminated but the process is always in place to prevent accidents from happening and danger to life and damage to equipment.

On the weekends, the owner of the company, who was a pleasant fella Mel, gave work for Josh and myself building, or should I say constructing, PLC cabinets at the workshop. The drawings would be single line in schematic form. This would incorporate drums of single core wire to wire up PLC inputs, outputs, relays, timers, switches, and transformers, as the control systems for the PLC telemetry are either 24v or 110v supply through the step-down transformer. This depends on the mine site as well. Coal mines and iron ore can have 110v controlled supply.

So, you can see if we weren't underground, we would be busy in the workshop, nose down, bumps up, building new switch gear for underground projects. We would also be point to point testing before gear went out . As my Irish friend would say, "To be sure, to be sure, to be sure," all the wires and connections were in the right place and no connections were loose.

Working on hoisting lasted six months as three of us were filling in for Glencore personnel who were busy on courses for the mine. We were called in as the few of us had experience in surface and underground mining operations as well as breakdown and repairs, assisting where needed.

Many instrument and engineering companies try to plan us in to cover shifts, or for maintenance shutdowns, electrical breakdown work, or mining construction.

In working this way, I have to carry electrical licences interstate, complete days of inductions and fill out paperwork for each mine. Every mine requires its own drug and alcohol screening as well as medicals and fitness tests. Fortunately, these are all paid for by the companies I work for as these would cost a fortune to pay for myself. The only real thing I have to do is turn up to the airport, bus, or mine charter and arrive, having been familiarised with the site and going to work.

We were finishing all maintenance and installation projects for Glencore, both surface and underground, and would be leaving Mount Isa once again to go to the Pilbaras in Western Australia to help finish the electrical construction project for Roy Hill Iron Ore mine.

THE ROY HILL PROJECT: A MINE BUILT ON A CATTLE STATION

The best way to appreciate your job is to imagine yourself without one.
— OSCAR WILDE —

We had finished at Mount Isa for the time being. We as The Flying Tradesmen still had the rental house out there as Roy was still under the apprenticeship training organisation and he would be working supervised with other contractors till I could get back and work alongside him.

Roy is not just a partner, a work colleague, Roy has become a good reliable friend. If I was away on maintenance or projects, we would always be in contact by laptop or phone.

Roy is very smart with technology-based equipment and is always trying to show me new skills on computers to try and adapt to this modern world. With his technology skills and my technical skills, we managed to make a number of projects happen as well as upgrade our skills and licences over the years.

My point of hire to Roy Hill Mine was from Townsville so I was paid to travel in company time and fly via Brisbane or Perth to Roy Hill mining airport. This mine and port facility is owned by one of the richest women and her family in Australia, Gina Rhinehart, with majority ownership. This mine is a very large mine located in the Pilbaras. It would become part of the large group of mines behind BHP Biliton, Rio Tinto, and FMG iron ore mining companies in Northwestern Australia.

Gina had her own railway lines built from the mine to the shipping port at Port Hedland. Railway line is a 344 km run between the mine and the port. When completed, the mine would produce at full capacity 55 million tonnes of iron per annum and would upgrade to producing 65 million tonnes within the next three years. I again would be asked to help increase the facilities onsite to boost the iron tonnage in later years.

The project was run by Samsung, the Korean company that makes appliances, builds power generating plants, builds ships and now a mine. This was not a good choice because the company engineers they had never really study the Australian regulations and legislations for building mines from scratch. Having found that out later, the Koreans were not good on seeking or having advice given to them.

However, I was onsite and after the few days of site inductions, licence requirements and certifications up to date for terminating, we started construction of electrical switch gear and power systems. The company was part of the construction unit and there would be at least 2000 persons over the whole site, which included personnel working at the port facilities as well.

Because of the accommodation shortage at Roy Hill Camp, some companies were busing trades people from places like Newman, which was an hour travel either way. If you consider a twelve-hour day and one-hour either way travel, it makes a long day. This I have done on many occasions with other companies. Our company staff

THE ROY HILL PROJECT

had secure accommodation at Roy Hill camp. This camp is one of the better camps I have been on with modern facilities. Some camps have a swimming pool, a big gym, tennis and basketball courts, a theatre, a coffee shop and store. The room facilities are very good too with cable tv, and all camps have en suites in every room. Food is good although you will always get those who complain. That's the camp and a number of buses turn up in the morning taking personnel to different work fronts over the mine facilities under construction.

Working on day shift for the first month was with a team of electricians connecting and commissioning one of the main conveyor systems and weigh bridges.

Working under Samsung Management was so strange. It seemed as though there was no scope or careful planning. Long lengths of steel conduit and fittings scraped, as every cable in some areas of the plant had to be run in steel conduit. Everything was done three times before the Koreans accepted the electrical construction. With this being their way of doing things, there was a huge amount of wastage. Samsung had a deadline to meet to get iron ore

pumping to the port facilities, otherwise there would be millions of dollars a day in penalties paid out to Gina Rhinehart's Roy Hill operations in compensation.

Really it was not ideal. This would be some millions of dollars lost to various mechanical, electrical and engineering companies. Ours would be one of them in later months.

I had a team of persons under me including TAs. I also was working under electrical processing engineers to carry out installations of processing and air conditioning instruments. All their calibrations would be documented as required except there were lots of upgrades on the drawing documents. This we would find out later.

Samsung couldn't leave the site quick enough in the end.

The first four weeks went quite quickly but the fly out day after our shift didn't go down very well. We were at that airport waiting to fly out when the Qantas Boeing 737 800 series had a bird strike through the turbines of the engine coming into Roy Hill airport. All flights coming in and out of Roy Hill airport are mining charter aircraft, either Qantas or Alliance Airlines. Another aircraft had to be flown in from Perth. This would be another four- to five-hour delay returning to Perth and my connecting flights to the east coast Brisbane Townsville would be missed. Usually if flights arrive late in transit and are booked through Qantas, Qantas would make provisions to get you on the next available flight or book you into a hotel at their expense. This has happened to me on a few occasions. But this flight was booked through a company travel agent. So eventually getting on the second aircraft, flying to Perth and arriving late, I was told by Qantas that I had to rebook through the company travel agent. It meant having to ring company head office who ring the travel agent to rebook another flight and get confirmation at the check in desk.

The later flight would leave at 5 p.m. Perth, Western Australia time to arrive in Brisbane Eastern standard time at midnight and I would have to wait at the airport till 6:00 a.m. to catch the flight to Townsville.

Having not slept really from the night before, you can imagine I was both tired and grumpy (and apparently, I was one of the seven dwarfs).

The times I do fly now have a little comfort as I relax in the Qantas club and business lounge to freshen up.

I got home mid-morning the following day with my wife waiting for me at the airport to take me home.

When you have your weeks off, the first day or night, depending whether you have been on day or night shift, all you want to do is sleep. The hardest part is your family wants you to be around and you feel like a zombie for a day or two. When you do come around, it's nearly time to fly back to work again.

Many people ask me why I do it. Why don't I get a full-time job? Three reasons.

1) In this day and age, there is no such thing as a permanent job. Take a look all around. If the economy crashes people are laid off, many not knowing what to do. This is archaic thinking. I have learnt to rely on a great God for guidance and wisdom and also from great people whom he has placed across my path in these times of economic uncertainty.

2) With huge government debt around the world and more inflated numbers or currency printed, it devalues the currency of that country or any country. When numbers or currency are inflated, the cost of living goes up. When so-called earnings don't go up fast enough to meet the inflation, people work longer hours to achieve the same earnings as they are trading time for currency. Just an interesting fact, the value of the Australian dollar and I would say most dominant countries has devalued by 30% since 1968 so you can see why many people are having to work longer hours.

There was once a gold standard. One ounce of gold was worth one dollar. This aligned everything fairly. When the gold standard was broken in 1971 by then Richard Nixon, president of the USA, they just kept printing currency and printing and creating figures. Currency became invisible as we trade with it, not having any external value. One ounce of gold is worth now around $2628 Australian dollars compared to one ounce being equal to one dollar years ago.

Why am I telling you this? If we don't retrain ourselves to be educated on finance and let money work for us, we are always going to be slave to it. This includes me.

I have retrained and although I still work these long hours, I am hoping to re-evaluate my work position. As I said above, the best way to value a job is to imagine yourself without one. This can be read two ways. I would prefer the latter, imagining myself to not require a job.

3) Many of the fellas work these long hours just to give their families a better living standard at the expense of their own time and family time, being away from home.

The novelty does wear off, especially on very long rosters. Loneliness and depression can set in. Marriages break up, then there's child support, drug and alcohol abuse. With drugs and alcohol, we are screened vigorously every day before entering site. Everyone is advised that if you think you may be over the limit from the night before, you should conduct a breath test on the machine at the camp. If you are over the 0.00 limit, ring the supervisor . If you come up testing positive, you will be removed with no questions asked, possibly losing your job for it as well.

Many people rely on credit and debt to maintain a lifestyle. Banks make money on credit and debt which is very unbalanced and has been for a long time.

In this industry many fellas and women wish they could cover all their living expenses without having to be away from home to do it. Some do it just to get away from home but most wish they could spend more time with their spouses and their children.

Having to make the most of this lifestyle, I have got to work alongside some great people. In the fourteen years I have worked in the mining industry, I have developed some very close relationships with a network of fellas. We have been able to encourage each other even through difficult challenges we have faced at work and on the home  front. We are not always in the one mine, but we have our phones and other communications to make contact as we look out for each other where we can. You could say we are a band of brothers.

Returning to Roy Hill Mine for the second swing. I got there with no delayed flights going back, this swing working night shift. This would be one of the new iron ore crusher installations. I think there were three on the whole site. The areas were fairly well lit up with portable lighting towers across and around our working fronts. We were working from the top of the stairwell area of the crusher to the bottom. We were also installing the instrumentation and lighting controls at the top of the roam pad, which is where the haul trucks dump the ore to go down into the crusher, as haul trucks need signals to know when to dump ore through the grid.

One night two of the fellas decided to shift a trailer lighting tower, forgetting to take the boom down as they were going under a bridge. Well, the bridge stood up ok, but the tower lighting had just a little bit more than a bit of damage. It wasn't a good look for the company as there were inquiries into the matter.

Working nights takes a bit of getting used to. Your body clock has to change and for some people, sleep deficits can still be a problem during the day. With sleep deficiency comes mistakes so all the team has to look out for each other. If anyone is suffering from fatigue, he or she is advised to have a few moments stand down time.

During day shifts, heat exhaustion can cause dehydration. This is also part of our fatigue management. Drinking at least five litres of water is a must, especially in the warmer months. Work in shady areas, take rest breaks. Of course, not all work is outside. And the flies. If you have never experienced swarms of flies all day long all over, you go for a ride up to the Pilbaras. Fly face nets are issued vigorously for us.

As for the fellas with the lighting tower incident, I couldn't help but think about the song by Kenny Rogers.

This turned out to be more than a strange site working under Samsung, I can tell you that. Within three weeks on our second swing on nights, 2:00 a.m., we got redundancy notices. But the good thing about it is that we got a good payout after we left. I went home with a lot of cash in my pocket. And I could finish the Kenny Rogers song: *There'll be time enough for countin' when the dealin's done.*

Well, the dealin' was done, I was countin' my money and I wasn't sittin' at the table either but I was on my way home. El and M, the company I worked for, was owed money and Samsung was trying to get other contractors in to finish project work, leaving companies millions of dollars out of pocket. Not just electrical but mechanical as well.

Gina had a deadline for Samsung and if they didn't meet that deadline, penalties would have to be paid. I think it was the beginning of November 2015. I know what they did do, the contract I think didn't specify how much ore they had to send to the port, it was the plant had to be producing ore. That's how Samsung got around it.

On the way home, we were not allowed to take our tools back with us on the plane. I am not sure if this was a weight problem with a full plane load and everyone's tools or El and M didn't want to pay for extra weight on flight.

We had to label our tool bags as they would be road freighted back to the point of hire. For me that was Townsville, over 4000 km away. I knew I would have to take out my basic hand tools and place them in my personal luggage. I wouldn't see my tool bag for three weeks and that's exactly what happened. You need tools to work and without them, three weeks is a lot of downtime.

A few months later, I would back at Roy Hill Mine and Port on maintenance.

There were several problems with the plant, the wrong equipment had been installed by Samsung for the processing. That's all I will say about Samsung design. The upgrading and some changes would come in later months when Samsung was no longer in charge.

Confidence is 10% work and 90% delusion. I pretty much felt this way in trying to hit goals at Roy Hill. However, you are always learning from other people or company mistakes, at least I do, and you find better ways to achieve better outcomes.

WEIPA PORT
RIO TINTO ALCAN PROJECT
THE GULF OF CARPENTERIA

Never take life seriously. Nobody gets out alive anyway.
— SYDNEY J. HARRIS —

Flying back to Queensland and resting up for a few days in Townsville, I would be spending some time with my wife. The first week is good being home and then I start to annoy my wife a little although she enjoys me being there. I always look forward to lots of good curries and spicy foods that Vijaya cooks, seeing my closet friends and hanging out at the airport with some friends there as well. Occasionally, I would help some elderly friends with chores and electrical maintenance, generally enjoying the great atmosphere and warmth of North Queensland.

I am thankful for health and every blessing God gives. I enjoy passing those blessings onto others.

The joy of the Lord is my strength.
— NEHEMIAH 8:10 —

Within days, I would be flying up to Weipa via Cairns. Weipa is a mining town on the eastern side of the Gulf of Carpenteria Peninsula. The town was built by Comalco to house all their families, government workers and support people for its Bauxite and Kaolin operations. Weipa has the largest deposit of bauxite in the world.

My job up there was with a crew of electricians initially upgrading the high voltage mains network in the township as well as working on break downs for Rio Tinto Alcan at the port and shift covers.

Weipa is a very hot and humid place in the summer. At 6:00 a.m.,

WEIPA PORT PROJECT

you arrive with clothes soaked with humidity and I mean soaked, to a point where one of the young fellas would arrive to a pre-start meeting with his clothes straight out of the washing machine, wet, knowing that they would eventually get wet, it was so humid.

The company I was contracted to was Carpentaria contractors and they had several electrical contracts with Rio Tinto as I have mentioned.

Of course, we had the relevant inductions for site and street work as well as the arc flash and high voltage refreshers.

Rio Tinto was in the process of building a complete new mine from scratch to replace the existing bauxite mine. The contracts had been in the process of being signed by the top Rio Tinto CEOs who had flown in from Europe in three private jets. I was there the day these guys flew in, quite impressive. I was told when a number of top executives travel this far across the world, they cannot travel in one corporate jet only, as if one plane goes down, everyone goes down with it. So, three aircraft are required for the number of executives.

Anyways with the setting up process, the main contractors were Bechtel, a company I had previously worked under at Caval Ridge Coal, and Hay Point Wharf upgrade. This company head office is in Virginia USA and Carpenteria electrical contractors were upgrading one of their office blocks for their mining operations in Weipa. This would be part of our scope of work as well to upgrade all the electrical installations in the building.

The first two weeks up in Weipa was trying to get acclimatised to the extreme heat conditions and I must have been drinking at least 8 litres of water a day.

Our camp facilities were owned by the company and situated at the old hospital and our dining facilities we drove to in the township. We had our own transport for work vehicles allocated.

Again, I would have my cornet with me and would entertain the fellas at night before they had a few beers and then I would wake

them up in the morning with a bugle call. Got a few unwanted go away remarks but it was funny. Initially one the fellas had dared me to, and I gladly accepted his offer.

It was appreciated by some fellas who nearly slept in.

We had a park across the road where we played touch rugby when it was a wee bit cooler at night. You could not go swimming because of the crocodiles, believe me they are big up there. But what we could do in downtime was go sand dune riding either on quad bikes or four-wheel drive utility. I chose driving in the ute as two of the young fellas came off the quad bikes and seriously hurt themselves. One fella riding in shorts and sand shoes got his leg caught in the chain of the quad and peeled the flesh right back up his leg. It was horrible to look at and he, being bandaged up, was taken to Weipa hospital and then flown by flying doctors to Cairns base hospital. The other fella Simon didn't do much better although his skin tears were able to be managed by the doctors at Weipa hospital.

Getting back to our beach joy riding, we lowered the tyre pressures in the four-wheel drive ute as the traction would be better

WEIPA PORT PROJECT

in the sand. Screaming along the beach front on the Pacific Ocean side of Weipa, we did manage to get it stuck in the sand and had to dig our way out. It did take a little time but we got out and pumped the tyres back up.

So, the following week, we were down two fellas for work. As you get older you become more aware of looking after your health and you don't take as many daring risks.

Still working these long hours in and out of the heat, I was able to manage my fatigue.

The owner of the company was a marine skipper who had a very expensive catamaran for salvage operations and heavy marine equipment removals. He also had a government contract in the past to scuttle illegal fishing boats that had been confiscated in Australian waters. Lenard, I will call him, also had a barge in tow. He would ship equipment around the coast from Cairns for both company and Rio Tinto operations. He had wharf facilities at Cairns as well.

He and his wife's rental portfolio was quite impressive. Some of the permanent staff rented some of these facilities and other rental accommodations were available for workers in the area.

His wife, I will call her Pam, was a helicopter pilot and flew a company JetRanger helicopter. I will tell you later about flying in and out of mining camps with Pam.

I was also installing all the HV equipment in Weipa township for Rio Tinto. (Bit of information for you, the Queen of England Elizabeth has 52% ownership of Rio Tinto).

I was checking tailings dams and having to wear a life jacket as I went near the water pumps on the pontoons. These dams were located remotely so I would drive the mining roads to them.

I would have a Rio Tinto female apprentice with me doing preventative maintenance checks from switchboards, substations, conveyors, building checks as well as sewage plant maintenance for the site and township. Also I got the odd call out for maintenance at Rio Tinto housing. I would be fixing machinery and equipment at concrete plants and their programs, also working on the Rio Tinto wharf repairing the electric mooring winches. We did everything, the young apprentice and me. She was a good apprentice. Some fellas find it hard to work with female apprentices, even me, but she was good.

This was a four-week swing, then home for seven days, with every Sunday off. This was good as I could join a church fellowship, which I did. I played my cornet there as well. Love music. It soothes the soul.

There were some good walking areas in and around Weipa as well. A lot of fellas had boats and would spend the days off fishing, coming back with big catches. Only problem up at Weipa, the rivers that feed into the coastline are full of crocodiles that guard their territory.

The Township of Weipa is a thriving community. Even in a downturn in the Australian economy, Weipa still manages to thrive. As Rio Tinto still owns a good percentages of the houses up there, power reticulation systems, with the high-quality bauxite and ships coming in, loading and going continuously, it keeps its community with continued employment.

Families come and go as people make their money from mining operations. Some stay and buy housing in the community and create private businesses, then make their money from supplying Rio Tinto mining operation with labour and tendered contracts.

The time I would spend up there would be from October till end of December 2015 on the first swing, home for Christmas that year.

In January 2016, I was asked to go back to Weipa. Initially, the first two swings would be completing maintenance contracts and HV cabling. Then after the first two swings, I was asked to come back and be a marine electrician onboard a dredge that had been

WEIPA PORT PROJECT

brought in from Singapore. Carpentaria contractors had been asked to supply an experienced electrician holding an MSIC for overseeing dredging operations on the river feeding to the port. The dredge was used to deepen the river as the build-up of silt and mud over a period of time had accumulated. A special ship would be coming into the harbour basin. A ship that had been working in the Middle East which would be cutting and removing the seabed for shipping operations in the harbour basin. Again, this is done to deepen the port for shipping as build ups of silt and sand, causing a shallowing of the port.

This was a very interesting ship as I had done all the marine inductions and training for the dredge and this ship. This ship would actually build and formulate wharf facility break water barriers as well. So, it cut, piped out the sea bed, and could also build reclaimed land with seabed removal and I did all this training. I waited two weeks, filling in with other projects to find out that the company that I was contracted to would not meet the Union award rates specified in the Rio Tinto contract and to my disappointment this work never happened for me.

In between times, I was flying out to the company mining camps to fix generators and earthing faults.

The workshop mechanic and I teamed up to be flown into these remote camps in a chartered aircraft. Ben checked and ran the mechanical side of generators, and I fixed the electrical system faults. Ben even came and gave me a hand when he had finished, having spent half a day checking, running and maintaining these generator systems.

The diner at the mining camps provided us with meals in between their usual allocated times of the fellas coming and going to work on different shifts.

This whole area as mentioned is full of high-grade bauxite, a big component of producing high grade aluminum.

When we finished packing all our tools, equipment and testing gear and ate our meal, we phoned Pam to come and pick us up in the company turbine helicopter.

It would be a three-quarter hour flight for her to arrive and land in the outer park of the camp. When Pam did arrive, we quickly loaded all our gear in, harnessed up, headphones on, then we were on our way. I didn't realise how small and noisy these things were as a rotary wing aircraft. As with a helicopter, it works in three dimensions. If you lose the back end, it goes into auto rotation and spirals. With a fixed wing, if you lose an engine, you glide comfortably and land. If you are flying a multiengine aircraft and lose an engine, you can still comfortably fly on one engine, or continue to climb with one engine failed and land.

Anyway, it was interesting flying low level over croc-infested rivers and near the coastline which spanned for kilometres. This is a remarkably harsh but wealthy in minerals country.

The more I see God's handiwork from the air, roads, and the waters, I realise this planet is an incredible place.

We landed at Weipa airport within the hour, helped Pam put the jet ranger on the skid platform and pushed into the hangar. That was it for the day for Ben and me. We placed our tools and equipment into the company vehicle we left at the airport outside the charter company and drove back to the workshop.

I had taken some photos as coverage on the way back just to prove I had flown in a company helicopter.

WEIPA PORT PROJECT

I would only be another two weeks up here at Weipa, by choice. The company had more work lined up, but also with the progression of the new Rio Tinto Bauxite mine with Bechtel as the main construction contractor, I had tenders out for projected work. So, there would be a substantial amount of work within the months coming.

My biggest problem working up at Weipa was not so much the work but the humidity. In Townsville and Cairns, it can become very humid but Weipa is at 100% humidity most days in the summer months. It was very tiring. In the last two weeks I would remain up there in Weipa, I reopened up some of the old mining camps that had been mothballed, testing the electrics to put the power back on as it been disconnected for some period, and working with Rio Tinto electrical inspectors to sign off paperwork and testing to ensure all electrical complied with the electrical regulations and standards before they authorised power back on.

So, in the next few months now, Weipa would become a mini-metropolis with a hive of activity as construction for the new mine would bring in a number of contracting companies and their staff.

I left Weipa in mid-March 2016 and would fly back to Townsville for a two-week break.

My wife needed me home for a bit to sort out some family issues. At the time, my youngest daughter Cilla had come back from overseas traveling and was living with us for a time. My oldest daughter Rachel was living with us all in our small apartment. Three women just about to kill each other. I was the only male in the house. When you work away from home, at times relationships are not always normal when you get home. You think you have done the right thing providing for and looking after your family, but your spouse and family crave your valued time and attention. I could come home to some very grumpy family members, in my case, three grumpy women. Family and marriage breakdowns can happen. I have seen it all around my working environment. Most of the fellas looked at

me thinking I have all the answers as I didn't seem to have problems as bad as theirs. But it did get to the point where I had to confide in someone else as I didn't always want to go home to face the problems. That in itself can have a devastating effect as you can form a relationship with someone else and end up hurting them as well.

To alleviate the pain I felt at home, I would spend the next few weeks in Western Australia doing inductions and working on BHP mine sites out of a township called Newman in the Pilbaras. I had kept in contact with this person and we formed a relationship for three or four months till something seriously happened to me. I had thought she had helped me through some painful experiences, walking and talking with her, and in between times, she herself had to go and look after her sick mother in Spain.

This is the next part of the journey. It felt as though I was not able to handle the issues. As a Christian, my trust is in Christ, to have no fear with his presence guiding me. But as the Bible says in Romans 3:23, *"All have sinned and fallen short of the glory of God."* And I am no different to anyone else.

WEIPA PORT PROJECT

I stayed away from home for nearly ten weeks. My wife Vijaya was very loyal but in those weeks was quietly grieving. She wasn't sure if I had walked out of our marriage. My youngest daughter, with the same temperament as Vijaya, was angry at me and Rachel, my quiet reserved daughter, just kept in contact with me.

I did fly back to Brisbane and stay with some family friends in that time. Arriving that day at the airport in Brisbane, I would see my friend off to Spain. This would be just before Carl and Jenny would pick me up from Brisbane airport. Of course, this would be on one of my weeks off, fitting in with an ANZAC commemoration weekend. My friends Captain Carl and Captain Jenny worked as ministers for the Salvation Army, attached to the military as RSDF (Red Shield Defence). There had been a military display. Karl and Jenny had been in attendance bringing me along with them on the Saturday. They loaded all the vehicles with items needed from Gallipoli barracks and went straight down to the Army unit display.

I did a lot of thinking over this weekend about my family and where my loyalties lay.

When flying back to work the following week, I was trying to keep myself together, working even harder and taking my mind off family and home. I was rostered on two weeks on and one week off with Lend Lease, a company I was contracted to for BHP. I would fly back to Perth for the week off, but on this one particular week, I had been able to organise getting on a maintenance shutdown at Nifty Mine. Without telling Lend Lease, I was working on my break having flown into Perth, flew straight back up to Nifty Copper Mine to do seven nights maintenance underground with a company called West Elec. Having done the seven nights and flying back to Perth then back up to Newman had a devastating effect on my fatigue management.

Our bodies are not designed to work continuously. The creator of the universe rested on the seventh day, seeing everything was good. I just didn't feel good having to work these long hours.

**My friend, remember without stupidity
there wouldn't be intelligence, and without ugliness,
there wouldn't be beauty.
So, the world needs you after all.**

The maintenance shut down at Nifty Mine was all underground. So, we drove down in two vehicles each day after pre-start. Our main objective was to clean out, test and relabel switch gear near the ore crusher and the two levels below where the conveyors brought the ore to the surface. We were going through isolation boxes for motor starters and field junction boxes for the PLC programs. There was another fella that had come with me from Newman who worked on the same shift as me. I liked to call him Big Brian from *The Life of Brian* (Monty Python). We worked together for those seven nights.

The crusher downstairs was not your usual flat vibrating crusher. This was a cone crusher, literally a cone with a mechanical driving gear which moved an arm around, if that's the best way of

WEIPA PORT PROJECT

explaining it. The fitters had this all in pieces as they were completely overhauling this in the maintenance programme. We were removing any electrics in the pit that needed to be taken out for the fitters and again would be installed when the crusher was reassembled.

We spent twelve hours underground for the seven nights to get the systems up and running by the end of the shutdown. We completed all that was asked of us and, coming off the final night shift, went back to camp, had breakfast, showered, packed up all our gear, caught the bus to the airport and the mining charter was waiting to fly us tired men back to Perth.

Most if not all slept and snored all the two-hour flight back to Perth. Landing in Perth would be a quick turnaround in the space of about three hours to fly back up to Newman. This was my downfall with physical fatigue.

I slept well that night and was up by 4 a.m. next morning for breakfast. There was a couple of times when over here in Western Australia, I had my watch alarm set to Queensland time. So, thinking it was 4 a.m., it was actually 2 a.m. Western Australia time. I had wondered for a few minutes why no one was at the diner. Figuring it out, I went back to bed for two hours.

This morning, I showered, had breakfast, grabbed our lunches and proceeded to our work vehicles. Having got in and searching for my security pass, I realised it was back in my room. Running back to get it, I tripped over a concrete tile. My boot had caught the top of an exposed tile and I went flying over, landing hard on my side. The damage was done. There was something wrong. By 9:00 a.m., I was in so much pain, I could not walk due to swelling. The fellas drove me back to camp for the rest of the day. That night, my leg was compacted with ice and I took Panadol to relieve the pain. I thought the swelling would go down over night but it didn't, it was even worse the next morning.

Management considered what they would do and made the decision to fly me home to see a doctor and rest up. Being in so much pain flying out, I managed to hobble up the stairwell to board the plane with some help. Sitting on the plane was very uncomfortable and it was even worse when we got off the plane in Perth and I had to walk down the long corridor that miners walk down disembarking off the charter flights. It was a case of stopping every so often just to have a rest.

Finally, when managing to get on the transfer bus between terminals at Perth airport, Qantas made provisions to wheel me on and off in a wheelchair between Perth, Brisbane and Townsville.

Arriving back in Townsville the following day, a friend picked me up from Townsville airport and drove me home. It would take me two days before I managed to see a doctor. And when I did see a doctor and show him my condition, he nearly fell out of his chair. His exact words: "What have you done, I have never seen anything like it. I'm sending you for an x-ray." So, I went and got the x-ray, still hobbling. The next day, I went back to the doctors, another doctor saw me with the x-ray results, and he examined me, nearly falling out of his chair as well. His exact words were similar to the doctor who examined me yesterday. "What have you done, you need to go and get a cat scan." So, I was sent to have a cat scan. The results came back as I had formed a hematoma on my leg. This was due to the heavy bruising and swelling. It was literally black all the way down from my hip to my ankle. Within two weeks, it did go down, the bruising faded, and I did fly back to work.

In that time at home, I was with my wife and decided to spend some time with her away and start talking again as we needed to do. It's strange. Sometimes you have been with someone for nearly thirty years and at times there are things about your spouse you don't even know. We had issues to talk through and some of these issues were very painful, but we talked through them. You can love your wife and not know you love her. In the last four years, we have still talked through our differences, although times seem to have gotten a lot busier. Having still worked all over Australia from the coal fields to the hard rock mining, to iron ore mining and processing, I have been trying to keep my relationship going at home.

WEIPA PORT PROJECT

> *If A is success in life, then A is equal to X plus Y plus Z.*
> *Work is X: Y is play: and Z is keeping your mouth shut.*
> — ALBERT EINSTEIN —

Flying back to Western Australia, I carried on with the maintenance for BHP Whaleback Mine in Newman. This would last for another two months on a shift roster before I would be shifted onto a two and ten roster. (Two weeks on, ten days off). This would be Port Hedland at the Roy Hill iron ore shipping port with G and S Engineering contracted to Roy Hill.

There was a team of us electricians from G and S and our main job was support maintenance and onsite breakdown maintenance for Roy Hill Port. A year before, I was on the electrical construction for Roy Hill mine, at the same time as the port facilities were under construction. Now we were maintaining brand new facilities with a lot of Samsung faults that we began rectifying.

We began testing faulty equipment in the switch rooms, helping with the HV switching. The main conveyors that ran the length to the port loading the ships would have down times so as we could work on the control and power systems. We had the iron ore stackers and reclaimers, the reclaimers that load the ore onto the conveyors to the port and the ship loaders that distributed the ore into all the shipping holds to maintain VSD (variable, speed drives) to check and test which programmes we were running correctly. It was always a case of cleaning the iron ore dust out of switch rooms and switch gear that had accumulated over days of continual working. We would walk up and down or drive up and down the conveyors to make sure all the pull chord and safety functions were working, checking all the proximity switches at the end of the conveyors. There were other switching checks at the top of the conveyors and the train car dumpers.

As you can see, maintenance is continuous. Without maintenance shutdowns along the way, millions of dollars of production would be lost if the processing went down due to faults on the system.

We would do a week of days, weeknights twelve-hour shifts, and then fly home.

Some of the fellas lived in New Zealand and flew home straight after shift. Some fellas lived in Thailand and would fly back there after shift. I would fly back to Queensland. Several times, I would meet up with my wife in Brisbane and drive to the Gold Coast or Airlie beach for time off.

The advantage about the week off is that you could have time out somewhere if you wanted it.

Roy Hill port was a good environment to work in. We had our restarts, we worked around every part of the plant to the loading of the ships.

One of the funniest pre-starts we had was starting with the usual safety briefing, any issues staff were trying to address, the tonnage

WEIPA PORT PROJECT

of ore shipped out in the last twenty-four hours and the captain's call from one of the ships. The captain had partitioned the port staff as one of the little Chinese crew had gone missing; they couldn't sail without him and hoped we could please have a look for him. He had obviously left the wharf and gone off site. We hadn't seen him. Maybe he had run away, gone into hiding, was waiting to claim political asylum. But there are not many places you can go to in Port Hedland. Eventually he must have turned up as the boat did set sail. As the iron ore boats set sail on the tide, I think they sailed a day late.

Interesting to note with the number of ships that come into Port Hedland, they come in at low tide, only 25 cm off the ocean floor. They sail out on high tide with between 50000 up to 180,000 tonnes of ore on the tide, the tide rising up to 7 meters and maybe more on a king tide. As one ship goes out, there can be up to another thirteen ships moored out on the Indian Ocean waiting to come in, as I one day counted.

I counted at times around eighteen ships at a time being loaded from different berths.

BHP has a number of berths on Finucane Island and Nelson Point. You have Rio Tinto berths on another part of port, then you have the ships that are loaded up from the salt works. Other ships loading up zinc concentrate and copper concentrate are on the other side of the basin to where I was working. But the port is predominately iron ore, and the ships are massive.

Driving on the road along the port access is one way so traffic lights are at either end and radios are required before entering, with MSIC opening the port access gate on the wharf end. This was Roy Hill Port.

On the left-hand side driving up the port access are mangroves. Now at low tide the midges seem to come out of their hiding and swarm any unsuspecting persons. They are horrible, they are so small, but they excrete on your skin, and you come up in welts. Protective spray is always on hand.

We had the Kawasaki roofed quad cars to drive around as well as Toyota cabbed utilities for going to jobs .

The power structure at the port for Roy Hill was running off generators. The power line infrastructure was in the process of being built so generators had to be maintained and fuelled as well. There was another company that looked after this process and monitored the power generated. With loading, stacking, and running conveyors from transformers to substations and switch rooms, the capacity of power needed and generated was phenomenal.

Working on the port facilities worked out well as I was able to work on my instrumentation theory courses on night shifts in my down time.

On every shift, we had fellas from Schneider Electric who maintained the function and programs for the VSDs. Their roster coincided with ours except when they went on break. Part of their company contract was that they were still on call anywhere around the country or overseas. This one particular time, an old mate was called to a problem in Zambia, a copper mine. In the conversation on the phone, he advised how to fix the problem by resetting a switch. No, no, they said, they wanted him to come and fix the problem. So, he had to fly all the way over to Zambia to reset a switch, which took ten minutes, and fly all the way back the next day. He was jet lagged when he came back to Roy Hill with us on the next swing. It was kind of funny. Their company policy: if you don't like it, look for another job.

On my last swing week off at Roy Hill, I had gone back to Perth to do the technical persons qualification for the Western Australia electrical contractor's licence. It was a full week of assignments and tests for completion of the licence.

I had booked into a hotel at Joondalup north of Perth and hired a rental car for the week. My GPS came in very handy as I hadn't a clue how to get to the training facility. So I would spend a whole week in a classroom to go over the legalities and obligations of an electrical contractor in Western Australia. Most of the input to

WEIPA PORT PROJECT

the course involved electrical installations, calculations for current rating capacities for installations, cable sizes and strengths for installing above surface and underground and to top it off, I had to complete an assignment before the licence could be issued. Well, I was the last to leave the classroom in the afternoon every day and first to finish assignment. So, we were the first to get our contractor's licence.

In that week, I was notified we had been made redundant at Roy Hill Port. But all our tools were still up there in the port workshop. I made inquiries to get my tools to be sent to Roy Hill Mine, as that was where I was going next. Completing the week in Perth at the Technical Institute, I would proceed to fly up to Roy Hill Mine within a day or two, expecting to find my tool bag sent to the main warehouse. Well my expectations were too much. My electrical supervisor at the port advised that the storeman at the port store would send it on the train to the mine.

My first conversation entering the store was, "Hello, my name is Richard Stewart. I supposedly had a tool bag sent on the train from the port to you. I've come to pick it up."

The reply was, "Just a minute. Will check with the port." Then the response: "No, the supervisor at the port store said he wasn't going to put it on the train, he sent it on the bus."

"Ah, ok, where has the bus gone?"

"To Perth," he said.

"Hmm, I'm at Roy Hill and my tool bag is in Perth. My tool bag will be sent up here to Roy Hill Mine and I'll be back to Perth after this shutdown."

And that's exactly what happened. They had to send my tool bags back to the G and S engineering office in Perth. By that time, I had gone back to Queensland and would have to make a special pilgrimage across to Western Australia to collect my tool bag a week later as the company would not freight it back. Fortunately, I had another matter to attend to in Perth.

With a lot of traveling and working, at times you expect things don't always go to plan. Most times I see the funny side if I'm not too tired, but common sense in many cases seems to have been thrown out the window.

I would be back in Mount Isa for a few weeks after leaving Western Australia, working on some cattle station maintenance. Many of the cattle stations were suffering from severe drought and we were still able to help them out with our electrical services. The station managers and owners were very appreciative.

Roy was also coming to the end of his apprenticeship and we were moving between Queensland and Northern Territory borders, either flying or driving. It would probably be our last number of flights in the plane before the plane would be flown back to Adelaide, South Australia. We had flown in for a maintenance shut at Ernest Henry mine and then flown up to Cairns, back to Mount Isa, and then back to Townsville. Roy would drop me off in Townsville and fly the plane back to South Australia. The distance covered by this aircraft was phenomenal, having covered the lower part of the Northern Territory and crisscrossing Northwest and North Queensland consistently. There is a lot of nothing out there in Queensland with cattle stations making up hundreds of thousands of kilometres as far as the horizon stretches. GPS is a must out there. In the months to come, we had literally run out of work for the plane due to drought in Northwest Queensland. To keep the aircraft sitting at Mount Isa not doing anything was a cost and also the extreme heat towards the end of year can have an effect on the physical condition if the aircraft is not being used. This is not to say we won't bring an aircraft back into service in the not-so-distant future. We may need a plane for emergency runs where the need is great.

Roy managed to organise some work with a company in Northern Territory just to finish off his apprenticeship. The apprenticeship training organisation was closing down and would have left him in a predicament. This would have messed up our work in Mount Isa as well. But he was able work in Northern Territory for a company

WEIPA PORT PROJECT

in Tennant Creek. Roy had arranged payment through The Flying Tradesmen; they would be his host company and pay his salary. Roy would be given work fronts way out in Aboriginal settlements as not too many of the other fellas who worked for this company would go out there too often. Taking a four-wheel drive vehicle, driving 1000 kms, sometimes camping, sometimes overnighting, but he did that work, and he did the hard yards when I wasn't around: changing out smashed electrical appliances, working on upgrading switch boards, replacing fittings that had been broken. Roy would always be in contact with me if he had any electrical problems and would facetime so I could identify the concern. Sometimes I could be around 2000 km away but with good reception, we could sort the problem.

To this day we keep in contact with each other if in different parts of Australia and meet up every so often, sometimes in Adelaide but more often Queensland. I am really proud of Roy and what he has accomplished. I can also say I have prayed for his protection anywhere he goes as he has been a faithful young man and has a good sense of humour. I hope he will continue on with all his achievements to benefit others as well.

Because we had a Western Australia contractor's licence, we had a certain number of jobs in the Perth area. If Roy got work through friends, I myself would go see them since I was the technical person under the licence. Some of his work was installing split systems heat pumps, which I myself did not have a ticket to install, but I could power up the supply to the units.

So, Western Australia has played a major part in work for The Flying Tradesmen as well as Queensland.

> *If you do what you always do,*
> *you'll get what you've always gotten.*
> *Go with the choice that scares you the most,*
> *because that's the one that's going to help you grow.*
> — ROBERT DOWNEY JR —

The second time I was asked to help out an electrical maintenance shutdown at a copper mine in the Pilbaras of Western Australia, it was quite interesting. Sky West, operated by Virgin Airlines, were the mining charter for the mine at that time and early that morning, we flew in to start the night shift. Flying in early gave us time to check into camp and have a few hours' sleep before dinner and then off to night shift. We were working underground again near the rock crusher and further below on this swing.

The belt splicers had been working on the main conveyor belt. The belt has so many hours life expectancy and then would be completely replaced due to the harshness of the ore product that comes out of any mine. Belts tear and burn, which is the worst-case scenario. If they burn, they can catch fire all the way up the conveyor. I have been where they have had major fires from this happening and damage to infrastructure can be devastating. The costs to repair and replace can be in the millions.

Every conveyor belt has belt drift switches on either side all the way up the belt. If the belt wears and drifts over to either side, it will activate a roller switch and stop the conveyor. Also, there is what they call a belt rip switch; if the belt breaks a wire, the belt is pulled down and activates a switch that stops the conveyor.

WEIPA PORT PROJECT

This night before going downstairs, we had done all our pre-starts and safety briefing. JHAs had been signed and all isolations had been made and lock boxes secured with all our personal danger locks on. The belt splicers rolled out 4000 metres of belt, having removed and replaced the old belt with the new. This was just before we were about to go down the decline in the work vehicles. They winched the return part of the belt, having the top part secured to splice both ends when the winch slipped. Four thousand meters of belt went straight down the decline. If you can imagine the weight, the force and the impact this would have at a speed going down the decline. This caused severe structural damage and fortunately no one was killed.

The underground was shut down for the whole shift and we couldn't do much as a safety investigation was in the processes. We basically sat around all night waiting for the final outcome, which we wouldn't know till the day crew came in the next day.

The structural damage would not stop production and the belt was winched back up. The contractors who had been working on this would have been scrutinised thoroughly and I'm sure the person in charge would have had some disciplinary action given him.

The company did get the belt spliced and joined again successfully.

As I said, the structural damage was significant as of the bent frames of the conveyor. Had anyone been standing near those sides where there was significant damage or at the tail end of the conveyor where the belt had piled, persons would have been killed instantly.

The day after, we were cleared to go down the decline as road access was clear. We actually worked on the feeder conveyors to the main conveyor, checking the motor drives, the counters, and control systems to ensure that when everything started up again, it would run satisfactorily. There are also weightometers that measure the weight of ore on the belt. These have to be recalibrated every so often to ensure correct weight outputs are calculated. Just like with flow transmitters or pressure transmitters, you want to know the correct flow or the correct pressure in the lines. If you get an imbalance in any of these figures, your production figures can be incorrect.

Process instrumentation is consistently being monitored by operators or technicians to ensure correct flows and tonnage are managed and this can be done by visual monitors with complete plant layout on desktop screens.

Copper concentrate is trucked out to Port Hedland where I think India was still one of the main clients. There the Indians would smelter and use the electrolysis system like here in Australia to grow the copper onto sheets.

The mining company had bought the mine and assets in Western Australia and Queensland off this Indian company in recent years, trying to increase production and supply for its clients.

Again, this was a maintenance shut and we had a time frame to get mill and production back up and running as the ore supply chain was from underground. Heavy earth moving machinery had a big part also in bring ore to surface and when driving underground these haul trucks had right of way. We would at times be turning into designated off roads to let them pass.

I would be back here again over the next few years, helping out here with shift covers for fellas taking leave or general maintenance upgrades.

By the end of 2016, I would once again be working underground at Mount Isa Mines and George Fisher, 20 km down the road. This time I worked on HV terminations, air refrigeration plants, and upgrades to HV switchyards. This was a big turnaround coming back from the Pilbaras and once again working out at far North Queensland.

I arrived back in Townsville for a few days, my wife barely recognising me, and was able to regroup and have a bit of a rest. In a week, I would be on the flight to Mount Isa. The accommodation spent out at the Isa would be with my teaching friends Bob and Debra. A spare room was available, and I was very appreciative of it. Bob was a Manuel Arts teacher at the Catholic college, a true Scotsmen and an inventor. Give him a mechanical idea and he would have a working plan to build machinery in no time. Give him a bit of wire and he would have a plan to fabricate a key within minutes.

Debra is a teacher's aid, a lovely lady, very caring, family oriented, always ready with a listening ear or to help where help was required. Bob and Debra planned to be in Isa for a period of time before retiring and going back to South Queensland to live.

Their lovely home was my base for coming and going for the next few months. This was not very far from the workshops and the mine site. I had a Honda 400 to ride to work on. I called it my imitation Harley as the design was similar. Not having ridden a motorbike for some time, I overcorrected myself one day going round a tight corner and nearly lost control, landing up on the other side of the road in the ditch. Fortunately, there had been no cars coming and I managed to steer the bike back on to the right side of road without losing control. I never told Bob this as this was his bike. I just know God's angels are there and am so thankful for his presence.

Once again at Mount Isa Mines, I would go down in the bowels of the earth, this time maintaining and installing power for essential services. This I would be working on for a few weeks on all levels of the Underground. The 11000v cable for mains power is very heavy cable and when jointing and running, it can be an all-day exercise. When finished jointing, we had to test the cable with insulation and resistance tests on high voltage electronic testers to ensure the joints and terminations had no faults, insulation was of high standard and visually there was no deterioration on the outer cable sheathing. This could take between four to six hours to be done properly. These upgrades on substations on different levels would be a priority for production. When working with very high voltage supplies, you can never be complacent. Power isolations and testing for dead are the priority. Then permits to work issued by authorised permit issuer. The permit issuer is briefed on the work area and what isolations are for, then the permit holder is responsible for the permit and every authorised person to sign on and sign off when work is completed. Then comes the isolation points where there is a designated isolation officer who's locked with a specific colour lock and in charge of that lock box. Then everyone working on the system or equipment has their own personal isolation locks, locking on to isolation boxes or isolation points that have been specifically set up and refer to the machinery or equipment they are working on. This system works very well. As mentioned previously, if anyone breaches these safety requirements, they are not only endangering their lives but the lives of others. Instant dismissal follows.

You don't want to see the end result when high voltage explosions occur. When people are killed in front of you or equipment explodes in a substation, you will always have that picture of what happened for the rest of your life.

We were installing high blast chiller air systems for the underground at George Fisher mine 20 kms down the road from the Isa. Ram air is blasted down the decline by large electric motors and the refrigeration side, although there is a certain amount of cold air loss. The system does have an effect to keep areas that can be extremely hot underground a little cooler. Imagine the air temp on the surface at 34 degrees Celsius, underground those temperatures can be between 40 degrees and 50 degrees with high humidity without the blast air and the refrigeration cooling down there. This is what they call hard rock mining. The walls are rock, the ceilings are rock, and the rock absorbs tremendous heat and it can get a little uncomfortable.

With the installation of this chiller plant, it can be monitored and controlled from the operator's hub through a network system. The operator can see the outlay of the chiller plant just like a process system where pressures and water flow are controlled, and valves in the processing side of the ore plant.

Working underground doesn't come without challenging physical medicals. There are usually two medicals, one for surface and one for underground. If you are working both surface and underground, you must have two medicals. Medicals involve cardiographs, eye and hearing tests, blood tests, urine tests for any drugs in your system (if found, you wouldn't pass a medical anyway.) Every body function is tested. Then you are required to do a physical test with the occupational therapist, lifting weights, doing step ups and stretches and push ups and sit ups, balancing, climbing, stretching your muscles, completing a breathing test. They give you an extreme work out as the conditions underground may seem easy, but when you get down there, especially coping with heat and pressure, it can be very demanding. As I said for myself, cooling off in the substation air-conditioning or vehicle air-conditioning is a must, also drinking plenty of fluids.

Underground maintenance continued till late December 2016. It would then carry on commissioning a new chiller plant for the underground services, followed by the upgrade to the main high voltage switchyard for George Fisher mine.

> *When we remember we are all mad,*
> *the mysteries disappear and life stands explained.*
> — MARK TWAIN —

With the requirements for the electrical upgrades and power loadings, we would be following on in the main high voltage switchyard at George Fisher mine. High Voltage transformers, oil mounted circuit breakers, lightning arresters and civil construction of concrete pads to mount up graded switch gear would be ongoing for several months.

The 33000v lines for us to work in the area had to be isolated from incoming feeder lines as the secondary incoming feeder lines would still supply the site or part of the site.

Before entering these switchyards, everyone has to have inductions and understanding of areas that have barriers, usually by plastic chain and markings to isolate live power from non-live power, the dangers surrounding switch gear. Even cutting through underground earthing grids can be a life-threatening situation due to inductance or leakage voltage flowing through the grid.

The gates as we enter are closed and locked behind us as we go in with equipment, vehicles and cranes. Plant equipment such as cranes or elevated work platforms must be bonded to a ground earth.

We found—in working the elevated work platform disconnecting the overhead droppers to the isolated transformers and oil circuit breakers—that although being isolated and grounded, we still had inductance or leakage voltage coming through the lines. Any power source is always tested when isolated. This is first priority to test for dead. Unfortunately, when working with high voltage 33000v upwards, you are always going to get small amounts of leakage voltage no matter where the earthing points. When testing and disconnecting we are wearing some form of insulated gloves for this very reason.

Another safety aspect in working in these high voltage switch-

WEIPA PORT PROJECT

yards, we have what they call a safety observer. His job is to monitor a specific work crew. If there is a potential of danger, whether it be a possibility of coming into contact with live networks, overhead movements, or lightning strikes, he can stop the job and close the yard until he is satisfied there is no danger to life or equipment. He signs people in and out of the yard and takes full responsibility of that switchyard. In other words, he is the gate keeper. He is an electrician with high voltage training and switching experience.

This brings me to the next part of the story, involving a friend of mine who was in this position as a safety observer. I will call him Nicolas for the purpose of this book.

Three other electricians, an apprentice, a civil construction crew of three persons and myself were building the construction to all the footings and platforms for new transformers and circuit breakers under supervision. We had been stripping down this heavy switch gear under the supervision of our company and the client's engineer in the switchyard. Some of the redundant cables had also to be removed from inside concrete cable ducts. These ducts were enclosed with steel plate covers, which could be removed to access or install additional cables. The concrete ducts themselves were about 2.5 meters deep. All around us were insulated live cables that I and another fella had been working around inside this duct where there had been no additional isolations for these cables.

There had been two JSAs brought as well as an HV access permit we all had to sign onto and sign off at the end of day for this switchyard. With the JSAs, one was for electrical and the other was for the civil works.

Now the electrical standards say only one safety observer shall be designated for one work group and we had two.

Nicolas could not see us in the enclosed trench, and he was supposed to be overseeing one work group, not two. Nicolas brought this concern up at the safety meeting and suggested the client needed to clarify their responsibilities as his electrical licence would be on the line if anything happened or someone was killed, or some person came into the yard or left without his knowledge as part of the work group.

With the JSA, everyone must read and understand what the job scope is, the hazards and the responsibilities of each person to reduce the risk of any hazard before they sign on. This by the way is a legal document.

The contracting company gave Nicolas a very hard time as Nicolas wanted to know where he stood with two work crews. It was a fair enough concern. The contracting company gave him an ultimatum, if he wasn't happy to f—k off. This he did. He left.

The next day Nicolas went to get his time sheet signed by this supervisor, only to find his Cadex or security card for access onto the mine site had been cancelled.

This really was unfair dismissal for bringing up a safety concern as well losing income. Safety concerns are promoted by companies not demoted at the expense of the employee. Nicolas had every right to forward this safety complaint to the mine's inspectors. This he did. There was a big investigation that went on for some months. I would be called in as a witness and the management I was also working under wanted me to take over the position, having summarised a layout of the yard and Nicolas's concerns by a written document.

Their first statement to me is that they were the contracting company with the contractor's license. If for any reason some person was injured or equipment was damaged, they would be responsible. Remember Hay Point, where I had a similar experience? If anyone is killed or equipment severely damaged, the person in charge of the switchyard is held directly responsible and I assured them of this.

Meanwhile, the civil contractors were not happy with the situation either and Nicolas had made a valid point for them as well.

Having reviewed this whole situation, I was not happy to continue with the company's policies. The acting supervisor and his henchmen gave conflicting stories, and this made things worse.

When the yard was closed temporarily for investigation, chains, gates and other items had been rearranged, which again would give conflicting information to a mine's inspector. Everything was supposed to be left as it was to evaluate the situation.

This investigation would go on for another three months. Management told me if I left, they could not guarantee work if I came back. This didn't faze me as I had other work lined up in Western Australia, building the electrics to new iron ore crushers in Western Australia. The best thing about consolidated heavy industrial electrical experience with interstate licences and tickets, you can pick up work and fit into most mine sites or heavy industrial plants.

In June that year, five months after the complaints were made by Nicolas, the mines inspector from Mount Isa wanted to fly into Townsville. Also a mines inspector from Brisbane would fly up to Townsville to give me a full recorded interview. Remember the mines inspector, whether they be electrical, mechanical, environmental, or chemical have the power to shut a mine, rig, or gas plant down until all requirements are satisfactorily met. If they see fit, they can do this.

So, this day in June, I agreed to meet them in a government office to go through with this interview.

The first thing they pulled out were signed copies of two JHAs and asked me if I had seen these. I said yes as they both had my handwriting on them. They proceeded to ask me questions about why this investigation was necessary.

We are dealing with extreme electrical dangers all around us for the upgrades. Everyone needs to go home safely every night. Aren't the standards and regulations there to protect and make safe every person working in this vicinity?

Theses fellas weren't policemen; they wanted my perspective of the situation. They were also interviewing one of the civil contractors who had gone back to the UK. So, for two hours nonstop in a recorded interview, I gave them every detail I could think of. They thanked me and eventually a report was made on the findings.

> *Those who hope in the Lord will renew their strength,*
> *They will soar on wings like eagles,*
> *They will run and not grow weary,*
> *They will walk and not be faint.*
> — ISAIAH 40:30 —

Over these years working in this industry, I have relied on this promise of above. We all grow weary of life. Life is tough, it can be a battlefield, but it's our attitude that makes the difference.

Like Winston Churchill said, *"Attitude is a little thing that makes a big difference."*

The next few weeks after leaving Mount Isa, Nicolas would return to underground coal mining and I would be back at Roy Hill Mine in the Pilbaras, Western Australia. Roy Hill Mine was wanting to increase their tonnage up to 60 million tonnes per annum and we were part of a team installing the electrics to these new small crushes and commissioning in new substations. This was in February 2017. I would spend a good month working on these small crushes for increase in production output for Roy Hill Mine. It seemed like every month, I would be flying many air miles for work.

> *"The road to success is always under construction."*
> — LILY TOMLINSON —

Within a month of finishing this small project, I was asked by an engineering company if I would be interested in being the electrician/operator on a methane gas plant in the coal fields of central Queensland. I had all the requirements, I just had to complete the medicals and inductions for onsite and there were a lot of inductions and training.

This is a methane gas drainage plant above the underground coal mine in central Queensland. The gas was processed and

WEIPA PORT PROJECT

piped through to the power stations that had gas fired turbines that pumped power into the grid system or power systems. The gas plant had five flares that burnt off the excess gas as well as field gas wells and water wells that drained off water from down below the ground level.

Our job was to monitor, maintain, and install new equipment where required; and sample the gas levels out in the field every two hours, registering the levels of oxygen and methane gases. These gases had to be below a certain level. These gases would be extracted by inserting a bag over a valve, opening the gas line on the pipe. This bag would be sealed, taken back to the office to be analysed at the main office lab. If the levels of gas became too high, the risk of an explosion occurring underground was very real; all personnel would be removed from the underground immediately.

Every piece of electrical equipment in underground coal mining is designed to be what they called intrinsically safe electrically. These are designed for arc flash or any sort of ignition absorption. We as operators had to have the Hazardous Area course completed for this work. The certificate itself lasted five years. Instrumentation was also a requirement for setting up plant PLC programs and being able to monitor the plant from every aspect on the control system—from maintaining the pressure of the flow of gas, the level of gas, the burn offs of gas and the drainage as required. Remember everything is very flammable when it comes to gas. If the gas volume or any part of the plant goes down, a call from the power station will come very quickly to ask what the problem is with the output of the methane gas flow.

There were usually four of us on days, including a supervisor, fitter and a programmer. On nights, it was just the two of us electrician operators. When starting with the company, familiarization with the plant and the field wells was a priority before going onto nights. We would connect new field wells during the day, commissioning and testing them. The wells had been drilled and piped for us to run cables to a powered switchboard and the programs would run remotely off a signal aerial back to the server.

This was one of the cleanest mining jobs I had ever known. The mine itself was on a fairly large cattle station, so the owners would receive royalties as well as rehabilitation of their land over the underground coal. I think they were paid to rehabilitate land themselves, which was another bonus for them. Healthy cattle also ran around, as the area was very good grazing.

When it came to sampling the wells at night, this was big open country with wide mining roads. It was ok finding your way around during the day but at night you could get lost.

Most of the staff drove to the site from Mackay, Brisbane, or Townsville. The Glencore staff were housed in the township called Tiare, a little township two hours inland from Mackay. The young fellas I worked with drove either two hours to or from Mackay or five hours to or from Townsville or eight hours from Brisbane. No problem for these young fellas to drive home straight after a night shift. I would stay and rest a few hours before driving back to Mackay and then flying back to Townsville. I had driven rental cars so many times

WEIPA PORT PROJECT

to and from the coal fields and was weary of hitting wildlife. I have ran over a snake sunning across the road, kangaroos, and dogs.

Driving back from gas plant to the camp one night, driving in a convoy, the fella in front hit a kangaroo and I ran over it, cracking the front spoiler of the car. One of the young fellas I worked with the day before hit a kangaroo and wrote his car off driving to work from the camp that morning. In the winter months, the warmth of the road seems to appeal to the kangaroos. An unsuspecting driver can have his car demolished in a short space of time if not protected by bull bars. Other dangers are stock or cattle wandering outside the farm boundaries. Cattle are more dangerous for vehicles to hit due to the sheer size and weight, the damage to vehicle and life are severe. Sometimes driving back to the coast, you would encounter heavy land fog for kilometres. So, you would have to be more cautious when driving.

Back at the gas drainage plant, I was learning more about the processing and flow of gas, and the field wells we were installing and monitoring pressures. I was driving out to the field wells and maintaining the burn offs. In between times, I was studying for my instrumentation courses. Being in the field, I was able to observe the processing and drawing of gas firsthand.

What happened next came as a bit of a shock to all of us in our crew. A company that had maintained the field wells for the last ten years had lost a contract and we as the electrical team "didn't have that much to do," as the bean counters thought. So, they would save the company so many millions of dollars a year and we would maintain these field wells with our workload and no remuneration pay for the extra work. Well, you know how well that would have gone down with every dual trader electrician. On the spot, two of the younger fellas were on the verge of leaving. Eventually they did, after me.

I had a little unfortunate incident coming off shift early one morning. Backing the Toyota ute into the car parks one morning in the dark, I backed into a fire hydrant and slightly bent it. Rushing to get all the paper logged into the system, I forgot to report the incident. There must have been two company employees who saw it and dubbed me in. It wasn't till after I had arrived home from shift, I received a phone call from my company telling me that an incident report had to be filed by me. If I had been a mining company employee, I would have just got a smack on the hand. But as an engineering contractor, those rules don't apply. It was an easy enough thing to do in the dark with no reverse camera and no protection around the hydrant. The frame was slightly bent, but because I had not reported the incident, they decided my services were no longer required. *Ok*, I thought, *just when I was beginning to enjoy the work and build up my experience in the gas fields*. The other fellas didn't stay long either and they had been there about a year longer than me. That meant the mining company had to train up more electrical operators at their expense. Who was to say how long these fellas would last if the expectations were very unreasonable? If companies want their staff to be loyal, they must treat them with a bit of respect and give them some incentives to stay. So often it seems one-sided, just about the mighty dollar. If a company is not making enough profit for the shareholders, they cut expenses or any areas to save money at any cost, and usually this is in the maintenance staff or projects. What eventually happens, the maintenance falls way behind and when it comes to the crunch, mining companies must spend more shareholders money to fix the problems than when they cut back on money to save a few dollars. Sometimes I wish these cost-cutting yuppies in their little or maybe big offices would come out into the field and get a little dirty to see how mine production works. This has happened in every mine I have worked on. The tragedy of it all is that after every maintenance shut, the amount of brand-new gear that is thrown in the bin as a so-called tax write off seems such a waste. The scrutinising of our work hours seems more important to them.

One thing we did get out of the company as the electrical crew, we were all given the Hazardous Area refreshment course in between all this. It saved us a cost of around $2000.

So, you can see our workload was starting to mount prior to all the problems happening. And of course, management was always changing, which didn't help. At times I just wondered where common sense and understanding really was in dealing with day-to-day issues.

When you look at the mining, gas and oil industry, on a whole it goes up and down. You have to ride the wave of the good times to make your money and get out.

**WHY FIX SOMETHING THAT WORKS WELL WHEN IT IS NOT BROKEN.
YOU LOOK AFTER STAFF, THEY LOOK AFTER YOU.**

From about July 2017 onwards, I would be on shift covers or break downs at the copper mine in the Pilbaras. Maintenance is always ongoing.

The supervisor Andy at the copper mine was always glad to see me. I had been in and out of this mine for coming on four years, both on surface and underground. We always had so much to talk about, Andy and myself, not only the running and problems with maintenance issues at the mine but life in general. Andy was an ex-Navy man—well-disciplined, articulate and always willing to help if you had a problem. There was also a good electrical team to work with here as the copper mine was not a big mine, which made the working environment more pleasant to work in. The crew was small and the mine layout a reasonable size. Our mine inductions always needed to be up to date as well as our medicals, as safety and training department would have records of every personnel.

This week we were working underground. We were overhauling and relabelling MCC boards (Motor Controlled Boards). We would spend the next week and a bit working on these boards consistently identifying cables, testing, installing new labels and ensuring the

PLC cabling also matched the programs.

There was one slight problem. They had taken the portaloo up to the surface. To take a dump, it was recommended I find a nice quiet place out of the way. This wasn't good enough, so someone had to drive me all the way to the surface to get to the toilet.

Eventually when I did back down, I was given the name the "shitologist." I am still reminded of this today.

It's interesting to note also that every underground mine has to have an emergency escape ladder system. So, every level down the decline is a hole made big enough for the largest person to climb, with ladders all the way from the bottom to the top. These must be maintained as the integrity of the ladders over the years can break down as was the case here at this mine.

At this stage, we were working on the surface when the replacement ladder was brought in and lowered by helicopter. The fitters had removed the old ladder system over the course of the previous three days so the drop could be made.

This mine would be around 1000 meters deep, so you can

imagine 1000 meters of fibre glass ladder hanging off a helicopter, being lowered carefully down the emergency shaft in order to replace the old steel ladder system. This was a sight to see.

The mines quite often use helicopters for very difficult lifts where cranes cannot adequately drop or lower loads.

On the surface also we were maintaining the conveyor and HV motors. The checks were part of the three monthly inspections. With the conveyors, we had the operators confirming we were opening and closing all the belt drifts and belt rip switches. Also, we recalibrated the weightometers. They measure the weight of the ore going up the conveyor before dropping into the stockpiles.

Walking up and down these conveyors to activate these belt drift switches keeps you quite fit. My step counter clicks me out on an average of 15 kms a day when on the surface.

CONTINUED

When we did get started, we built the circuitry for the PLC telemetry in the MCC (motor control cabinets) downstairs as well as installing and terminating PLC junction boxes on the first level walkways then two levels below where the conveyors moved the ore to the surface outdoors. It required wiring in new LCU (Local Control Units).

We had all our hand tools with us and all portable tools such as battery drill, grinders, lighting stands, etc, supplied by the company and the stores through Elvis the singing storeman who would assign these out.

As we were working with several different crews, some work fronts had priority over others. If cranes needed to be set up for heavy crane lifts, we would have to move. Our job front would be changed. *Never work or walk under a suspended load.* I have been where slings have slipped, changes have broken under the incorrect loading and people have been crushed.

Safety is taken very seriously and *if the job is not safe, don't do it.*

The five-week period has been planned to allow for enough man hours to complete the whole maintenance shut. If there are delays, which can be unavoidable, unnecessary work can be planned into the following maintenance shut.

When lifting is taking place or when mechanical, welding or electrical is on level as above or below a drop zone is initiated, barricading can be in the form of red and white tape labelled "do not enter without express permission from the area owner." Breaching this can be removal from site.

Other tape is black and yellow caution tape, labelled with details of work in area and reminding to enter with caution. There is another tape we use; it is blue and white. This is an exclusive controlled area. No person can enter this area, only those involved in prescribed work. Areas taped or barricaded off can be in sections or fixed areas.

When it came to testing electrical installations, the iron ore dust can be a problem. The congestion of dust over live electrical switch gear can short out and cause flash overs if not consistently cleaned out on designated shuts, electrical switch gear having been isolated.

I have seen the results of what dust collecting on electrical installations can do. At a coal mine in the last year in an MCC room, an upgrade was taking place with a new electrical cabinet being installed to run a new VSD (very able speed drive). On commissioning this installation, an insulation resistance test was only done without a duct or test done on the three-phase 400v busbars for the additional alteration. The electricians removed their isolations, went to switch on the mains breaker and there was a *boom*. The HV fuses blew, taking out the MCC room. There was damage but the main concern was that every circuit fed off those three-phase bars had to be disconnected to see where the flash over had taken place, due to coal dust build up. This would be at a cost of man hours and production.

On another site a few years ago, a project inside another MCC

WEIPA PORT PROJECT

cabinet was taking place. All the isolations and locks had been put in place and as the upgrades were taking place, one of the fellas dropped an uninsulated shifting spanner into the dust below inside the cabinet. The result was the zinc and lead dust immediately thrown up and tracked across the three-phase busbars downstream. The flash from the arc blew out at some considerable current and burnt the fella's arm badly. This was with all the safety in place. No one ever thought to write up in the JSA allowing for any dust prevention measures.

There was an investigation, and recommendations were immediately initiated.

Safety is a priority. The work will get done with the hazards minimised or, more importantly, prevented.

The testing would be completed. All the new systems were go. The electrical engineers were validating the new programmes and upgrading the existing programmes. With all mechanical and electrical locks and interlocks removed, a time of commissioning and trial runs of the carriage dumper would take place.

All we had to do was to be onsite working with the engineers, ensuring the functions of the telemetry were working as they should, and the SCADA programs could be acknowledged by all monitors. All the activations of gate switches or locking switches could be activated out in the field manually. To prove these when activated, a fault would light up on the program. To clear, remove the test object and the initiated fault would show as cleared on the program. We have access to these monitors in every switch room and substations as authorised electricians and engineers.

The day we finished we would pack up all our gear, clean up and go back to camp, ready to fly out the following day.

The next morning, I flew back to Perth, expecting to catch the 12 noon flight to Brisbane then on to Townsville. The flight coming in from Brisbane had been delayed due to heavy thunderstorm activity and was diverted around the weather, thus causing an hour delay. This would mean the flight out of Perth would be late leaving and connecting flights out of Brisbane would be missed. That's what happened. Qantas would once again have to put us up in hotels for the night and transport us next morning to airport. We would be on the first flight out to our home bases. Always good when there is no cost involved, only a few hours late home. My wife would be there again at the airport to pick me up and, as women do, express the joy to see you and everything else that's not working right.

One of the advantages of fly in fly out work is that you can take time out for a holiday in your down time. Sometimes I would meet my wife in Brisbane and go to the Gold Coast for a few days or meet Vijaya in Sydney, travel to the Whitsundays or Cairns. As I said a number of the fellas I have worked with lived in Thailand, New Zealand, even some in Indonesia, not my idea of home though except flying back to New Zealand for ten days would be ok.

I KNOW MY LIMITS, I DON'T ALWAYS OBEY THEM, BUT I KNOW THEM.

Towards the end of 2019, I would fly back to Western Australia to commission a substation that had been constructed on engineering premises at Canning Vale just out of Perth. I would pick up a rental car and leave at 5:00 a.m. to start work at 6:00 a.m. This new HV Substation had been built for Roy Hill Mine. It would be tested and put through all its functions by engineers calibrating all the telemetry and the dismantled in sections and transported to Roy Hill mine site up in the Pilbara.

My work with four others was point to point test all the cells and the cabinet functions on the MCC side of substation, secure and fix all the main earth bonding on the building structure and then help in testing all the HV switching on the control side with of course no high voltage power on, only the temporary control power. Working with HV switch gear and testing equipment is very rewarding work.

In six days, I made enough for my flight, accommodation, car and still had money left.

WEIPA PORT PROJECT

There were two more projects I was involved in before the end of 2019. The first project was flying to Western Australia and changing out three HV substations underground in three different gold mines that were between 500 and 600 km apart.

Arriving in Perth, I would be picked up the following day and taken down to the company workshop. A heavy vehicle with a 10-tonne HV substation had been strapped on to be wheeled down the decline to the first mine. We left late morning to drive the 700 km from Perth to Kalgoorlie. I drove the Toyota twin cab behind an old mate in the heavy vehicle. We stayed overnight at Kalgoorlie, and another team member flew in to join us that night and we would all leave the hotel together the next morning to drive the first 500 km to the first gold mine.

Arriving at our first destination (cannot give name of these mines as for sensitivity), I checked into the mining camp and got set up for the following day. We of course would have to do all the temporary mining inductions for the underground as we would only be there for the three days removing and installing the new substation.

The next day when all the inductions and sign offs were completed, we were ready to drive down underground, followed by the loader. We would isolate the power to the sub from switching station on levels above then disconnect the existing HV sub that was on skids and have the loader haul this up to the surface. The substation on the back of the truck would be lifted, placed on the ground, jacked up and wheels mounted on. The loader would tow this down to the level required. We would drive down ahead. By the way, we have to tag on before the entrance. This is security-related as your card identifies each person down the hole and every person is tagged out before any blasting can take place.

We would wait till the loader had come done and would give directions for turning the substation so the loader could move it into position on the concrete pad. Once on the concrete pad, the loader would disconnect; we then would bring the jacks out, jack up the wheels and remove them, lower onto the pad. Then we would connect up the HV leads, check the phase rotation was right and go back up to the next level and reenergise the power.

We would then go back down to ensure power output was reading correctly as this is a step down transformer from 33000v to 400v between phases. A bigger substation gives greater current capacity, ensuring that extra loading required down the decline is adequate for running operations.

Our job was done here. We would go back up to the surface, lift the HV substation we had brought up onto the heavy vehicle, strap it down and drive back to the camp, ready to leave for the next mine the following day.

About 4:30 a.m. the next morning, we would rise, have breakfast, be on the road just after 5 p.m. and drive another 600 km to the next gold mine. Same routine. Remember these mines were several kms off the main highway so we were travelling 600km plus the mining access roads.

We would try and have the inductions done the same day at this mine as we had to run nearly 100 meters of 1100v cable down three

WEIPA PORT PROJECT

levels from the switching point three levels up. This was very heavy work.

Again, we would have to lock on with new locks and ID cards, signing onto JSA, work access permits and HV access permits signed off.

Holes had been drilled by GPS coordinates down through the three different levels through the rock and we had this massive 100-meter drum of cable on the top level we had to pull out with our vehicle. The longer the cable is pulled out, the heavier it gets. So, each level we dropped it down, we had to measure by cable markings the required amount for each level. These amounts were given to us. We still had to clip cables to cage netting on the rock ceilings in some parts and down the underground access road. We would use a basket chained into the front forks of a heavy loader to raise two of us to nearly ceiling height. One of us would hold the cable whilst the other would clip it to the ceiling mesh. This was another good three to four days of work. This would also include terminations of the HV cable.

I did get to see one of the operators underground drive heavy machinery remotely from his hut. He had his monitor and joystick and then he managed to have a boulder drop onto the cab of the heavy earth moving machinery and got it stuck. He couldn't get it out. Never saw how they got it out because I wasn't there long enough.

We did power up this sub and check all the running functions. They worked perfectly. Job done.

The next morning, leaving around 5 a.m., we drove from the camp with an empty heavy vehicle as the next HV sub was waiting for the next installment. These HV subs were assembled in the company workshops and placed under test there.

We would drive the next 600 km via the mining back roads as we thought they would be quicker. They might have taken a few kms off the driving distance but they were really rough.

Driving onto the mine site, we accidentally drove over a Guiana and squashed it. These are protected wildlife. Fortunately, no one saw us do it. We would check the sub, ready to take down underground for the next day. We once again had to jack this substation up on wheels to tow down by heavy earth-moving equipment.

This would be a two-day exercise as we only had to take down and power up. The next day, having done all the inductions previously with locks and underground belts and lamps, we were ready to lock and tag on to go underground. All the work permits and access permits were signed off for us to go down. However, when we went to tack the sub up to place the wheels on, there was a massive Guiana living under there and he wasn't too fussed about us removing his dwellings. For a few moments, he would wander around until he realised he would have to find another shady spot and eventually he wandered off.

We had a bit of a hold up for about half an hour. I decided to turn my helmet cap lamp off. It was complete darkness. This reminded me of being back in New Zealand caving all those years ago with a group of fellas in a caving cavity and we were told to switch our lights off for a minute or two. *Complete darkness.* I am so glad for the sunlight as I would never want to live in darkness.

We did then get to remove the wheels, connect the incoming and the outgoing connections and go up to the upper level and power up the sub. Going back down, we tested all the functions and readings of voltage outputs. These were all good, our job was done. We drove back to the surface and removed our tags and locks. We gave back all our underground gear and the new underground belts the company gave to us. We signed off all the permits and cleaned the vehicles of gear, signed out from the lay down yard and drove back to camp.

The next morning, I would be driven back to Kalgoorlie, flying from there back to Perth and then flying back to Townsville via Brisbane. We would leave once again around 5 a.m. and be in Kalgoorlie at a reasonable hour. This would be a 400 km drive and I would be flying out at 10 a.m.

WEIPA PORT PROJECT

In the ten days we had been on the road, we had driven well over 3000 kms, and installed three HV substations in three different mines. We were a bit tired by the time we got home.

NO MATTER WHAT THE SITUATION, NEVER LET YOUR EMOTIONS OVERPOWER YOUR INTELLIGENCE.

Sometimes when I look back on all this work and travel, I wonder what's it all for, can't I just have a normal life? Then again, what is a normal life in this day and age? It's tiring and an adventure, it's lonely but it's been resourceful. It's been emotional especially when it comes to family. It's been rewarding especially when I have been there for the needs of my fellow workers. Would I do it all over again? No. I value the experiences but the more I journey through life, the more I see that people matter and family matter, not things, not money, although we need it to survive.

My philosophy now is to work smart, not hard, and in the next two years, I am going to prove that to myself.

The end of 2019, I would be back in Townsville setting up the infrastructure and temporary power for the new upgrade to the electrolysis plant at the zinc refinery, twenty minutes from home. We would be setting this up for a two-year project that employs a number of big contracting firms. The company I would be working under is with my old friend PDL electrical. I would be working with a nice indigenous fella by the name of Donald Beale. He looked just like Denzel Washington so I called him Denzel. Denzel is very intelligent and could hold great conversations on many subjects, a very open-minded person. Very dependable. He was a hard worker and had a nice smile and was very good at what he did. He also liked to joke around a bit. A very shy man though when it came to crowds.

The ground preparation and then the concrete infrastructure footings were being made up. In between times, we would be helping with the preventative maintenance from the Sun Metals

workshop to the whole of the plant and also the acid plant itself. In the sulphuric acid plant, we would have to wear full body protection and full face respirator protection to enter the area. Of course, all permits have to been signed onto and off at the end of day for particular areas .

Sun Metals also has other business ventures as I have mentioned previously with the acid trains going out to Mount Isa Mines, a fleet of trucks that bring in zinc products from Cloncurry and also supply transport for Mount Isa Mines lead ingots. Its main production of galvanisation ingots are shipped to South Korea. Townsville Sun Metals provides a number of jobs for skilled people, and for a number of Korean nationals who also work alongside them.

Not too far away from Sun Metals off the main road north to Townsville is the Glencore copper refinery, where the copper smelter tablets come in from Mount Isa Mines and through electrolysis the copper is processed and taken out in sheet form to be shipped out for the international markets. There was the nickel refinery north of Townsville but for various reasons, it is out of commission.

Townsville is a mining hub for Northwest Queensland hard rock mining and Central Queensland for coking coal for production of steel. Townsville is also home to one of the biggest deployment military bases in Australia. Many war games are played up here in the hills behind the military base and for the Royal Australian Airforce there are designated active areas when these war games are on boarded in red on civil aviation maps. These active areas can be seen on the outer parts of Townsville airspace. Although a military airport commercial and non-commercial aircraft are able to fly on a daily basis, usually for light aircraft if the military areas are active a NOTAM (Notice To All Airmen) is sent out and flights are

WEIPA PORT PROJECT

scheduled around these military active zones. I have encountered these detours on many occasions.

Lining up behind an Air Force F18 Jet is something special even if you have to wait a few minutes for the wake turbulence from the jet engine to dissipate.

Townsville is also a gateway to the Great Barrier Reef and many coastal islands that have a history.

If you lose the power to laugh, you lose the power to think.
— CLARENCE DURROW—

So, this was 2019 into this coming year 2020. No one could have known the events that would change life not just in Australia but the world, from horrendous bush fires that covered three states, wiping out communities, life, and animals to Covid 19, which has taken the lives of hundreds of thousands and infected millions. Covid has disrupted economies, causing stress on families, and people have been locked up in their own homes for weeks and sometimes months to prevent the spread of this virus. Transport systems had to stop running, airlines stopped running scheduled flights, borders closed interstate and nationally, and job security was lost by millions around the world.

As I write this, I am one of those who got locked out of my own state Queensland as I was working in Western Australia at the time, and the borders were under lockdown.

As a I write this chapter, I have been away from home nearly fifteen weeks and counting as initially my work front had been placed on hold. Queensland companies have not been able to get gear in from overseas holding projects and the industry up. The virus has put these same companies on full alert with employees. Even here in Western Australia as I write we have had to carry company documents as Fly In Fly out workers that say we are authorized to work in the areas designated. For me, that is Port Hedland and the Pilbara. These documents are checked before we board our flights, and we have to sign documents for BHP saying we have not been in or travelled to any overseas countries in the last fourteen days.

Our temperatures are checked by nurses before boarding flights. There have been some cases where personnel have been stood down, having been found as carriers or showing symptoms of the coronavirus.

For me now to fly back to Queensland, I would have to go into fourteen days of self-quarantine and if flying back to Western Australia, I would have to go into self-managed fourteen days of quarantine. To enter quarantine is pretty much a lot of down time for me so I have chosen to remain here in Perth and pick the two weeks on two weeks off roster and fit in any work in between. It's a chance I have had to take.

My two weeks in Perth, I stay at my friend Joe's budget hotel, as my friends out in the country side, who I would have stayed with, have been under lockdown as well.

Though all this, I am trying to keep my sanity, my sense of humour, encouraging and praying for those around me who are struggling, thanking those around me who have accommodated me (my friend Stephen). With the downtime I have had, I have been able to ring and contact all my friends and family around the world from England, Canada, USA, Australia, and New Zealand. Also, my friends back in Queensland—Frank, Ranga, Julian, Lindsay, Ian my Fijian friend, my family and my friends in New Zealand.

We are a Band of Brothers, and we look out for one another. Sometimes we feel an intuition when we need to contact each other to make sure every one of us is ok.

These are my friends my family as well as my immediate family. We share good times and not so good times.

I NEVER MAKE THE SAME MISTAKE TWICE.
I MAKE IT THREE OR FOUR TIMES JUST TO BE SURE.

CONCLUSION

As I conclude writing this book, I just want to thank my Lord and Saviour Jesus Christ who has shown me through every good and not so good decision. He promises, *"I will never leave you nor forsake you."* This I would encourage every person who decides to read this book, we all have a God-given talent unique to us. When you know what it is, you must use it for the benefit of others in this world. When people know you care, and they know they are not being taken advantage of, they will share and come alongside you. My friends here in Australia, New Zealand, and many other parts of the world know this of me.

The mining and resources industry is not for everyone. As I have mentioned it's tough, it's time-consuming, it's tiring at times working in the heat, it can be lonely, it's travelling, it can be adventurous, but it also can see its share of dangers and it has taken me away from family.

On the technical side, it has rewarded me with many new skills, taken me to many places around the Australian continent, improved my skills with dealing with people and made me more of a responsible person, taking safety and life very seriously. From here, I will move on to new adventures in the future.

— PROVERBS 3:5 —
Trust in the Lord with all your heart.
Lean not on your own understanding.
In all ways acknowledge Him and
He will make your paths straight.

PHOTO DESCRIPTIONS
plus Additional Photos

Page 1	Mount Isa Mine
Page 2	Safety equipment
Page 5	Termite mound
Page 10	Licenses
Page 11	Mary Kathleen Mine
Page 13	Driving underground
Page 22 TOP	Construction of gas turbine
Page 22 BOTTOM	Power station
Page 24	Solar farm
Page 27	Sleeping quarters
Page 28	Underground vehicle
Page 35	735 equipment
Page 36	Electrics in high voltage motor
Page 37	34-30 equipment
Page 39	Cat electric truck
Page 41	MCC switch board
Page 45	Mobile plant
Page 49	Townville Sunrise
Page 53	Overhaul of electric drag line
Page 56	Ore transport
Page 70	Flying into mining camp out of Weipa far north Queensland.
Page 71	Aircraft flown by the Flying Tradesmen north west Queensland
Page 86 TOP	The Downer EDI Crew Porthedland BHP I'm 7th person in from the front.
Page 86 MID-LEFT	Lunch

Page 86 MID-RIGHT	Ques at dinner—social distanced
Page 86 BOTTOM	Airstrip at mine
Page 88	Telemetry
Page 90	Underground tunnel
Page 95	Sunset
Page 97	Working Porthedland
Page 101	My friend Steve who put up with me in a hotel in Perth when I was caught between borders 2020
Page 106	Saturday off work in Weipa. 4 wheel driving got stuck on the beach
Page 110	Company helicopter
Page 112	Mining airport
Page 114	Underground crusher
Page 118	Iron ore stacker
Page 124	Iron ore conveyors
Page 125	Night shift break
Page 135	Power station
Page 140	MCC electric room
Page 145	HV substation
Page 150	Acid clothing
Page 152	Nurses checking us for symptoms of the dreaded Lurgi Covid before we were allowed to step on plane at Perth airport. 2020 to Porthedland.

— ADDITIONAL PHOTOS ON THE NEXT PAGES —

PHOTO DESCRIPTIONS & ADDITIONAL PHOTOS

TOP – Generator NQ Mines

BOTTOM – Underground sled

TOP - Iron ore ship

BOTTOM - Work in the bore fields

PHOTO DESCRIPTIONS & ADDITIONAL PHOTOS 159

TOP – Underground meeting

BOTTOM – Emergency shelter

TOP – Sunrise, Galilee Basin
BOTTOM – Sunrise, North Queensland Mine

PHOTO DESCRIPTIONS & ADDITIONAL PHOTOS   161

TOP – Sunset, Newman Mine

BOTTOM – Sunrise, Newman Mine

TOP - EOB repairs on truck

BOTTOM - EOB repairs on truck

PHOTO DESCRIPTIONS & ADDITIONAL PHOTOS

TOP – Working on ladder

BOTTOM – Bombsuit

TOP – Coffee break

BOTTOM – My friend Gregg and I

PHOTO DESCRIPTIONS & ADDITIONAL PHOTOS

TOP - Sunrise while flying to work

BOTTOM - Barrier Reef

TOP - ND City Harbor
BOTTOM - Skywest Plane

PHOTO DESCRIPTIONS & ADDITIONAL PHOTOS

TOP - Downtown Perth

BOTTOM - Perth police

At night at one side of Port Hedland looking over
the other at the iron ore shipping port on night shift.

www.ingramcontent.com/pod-product-compliance
Lightning Source LLC
Chambersburg PA
CBHW031249290426

44109CB00012B/502